# THE ALL-NEW
# REAL ESTATE
# FORECLOSURE
# SHORT-SELLING
# UNDERWATER
# PROPERTY AUCTION
# POSITIVE
# CASH FLOW BOOK

# THE ALL-NEW REAL ESTATE FORECLOSURE SHORT-SELLING UNDERWATER PROPERTY AUCTION POSITIVE CASH FLOW BOOK

## Your Ultimate Guide to Making Money in a Crashing Market

**Chantal Howell Carey and Bill Carey**

**WILEY**

John Wiley & Sons, Inc.

Copyright © 2009 by Chantal Howell Carey and Bill Carey. All rights reserved.

Published by John Wiley & Sons, Inc., Hoboken, New Jersey.
Published simultaneously in Canada.

*Library of Congress Cataloging-in-Publication Data:*
Howell-Carey, Chantal.
   The all-new real estate foreclosure, short-selling, underwater, property auction, positive cash flow book : your ultimate guide to making money in a crashing market / by Chantal Howell Carey and Bill Carey.
       p. cm.
   Includes index.
   ISBN 978-0-470-45586-9 (pbk.)
   1. Real estate investment. 2. Foreclosure. I. Carey, Bill, 1951– II. Title.
   HD1382.5.H69 2009
   332.63'24—dc22
                                                                      2009010885

Printed in the United States of America.
10  9  8  7  6  5  4  3  2  1

# CONTENTS

# PREFACE

Welcome to the greatest real estate money-making opportunity of our lifetime. The real estate market has crashed. For the bold and savvy real estate investor, *now* is the time to buy. Buy as much real estate as you can as quickly as you can and consider financing the sale as the banker for quick cash and cash flow or holding the property for cash flow and future cash profit. You will become a multi-millionaire if you do.

The United States government is proposing to pump $9.7 trillion into the economy over the next four years according to the *New York Post* (February 10, 2009). One trillion dollars will be in the form of an economic stimulus. Three trillion dollars will be in the form of lending and spending programs. Another $5.7 trillion will be in the form of agreements to provide loan guarantees or aid to various entities at home and abroad.

How many trillions will go directly into the real estate and mortgage markets has yet to be seen. The indirect impact of all this government spending on the real estate market is huge. Real estate prices will be going back up. Inflation, not deflation, is in the pipeline.

## Strategy

You must have a strategy in order to make money investing in a crashing real estate market. Some investors use a quick cash strategy to buy and flip properties immediately. Some investors use a long-term wealth building strategy to generate cash flow and hold properties for future appreciation. We recommend you use both strategies. We will show you the pros and cons of each.

## Foreclosures

Twelve million foreclosures are predicted to occur in the next four years. In Part One of *The All-New Real Estate Foreclosure, Short-Selling, Underwater, Property Auction, Positive Cash Flow Book* we present the all-new investment tactics needed to take advantage of this foreclosure bonanza. These new tactics include coupling short-selling and auctioning with the government bailout of the residential real estate mortgage and housing industry.

We will show you why it is in your best interest to stop buying foreclosures at the white elephant sales (the courthouse steps). We will take you inside lender loss mitigation departments and show you the 12 factors that a lender will consider before accepting your short-sale offer. We will also show you how to buy the mortgage in foreclosure from the lender at a short-sale discount.

## Sellers Are the New Bankers

In Part Two we present what you must do over the next four years to become a multimillionaire investing in real estate. This starts with understanding that in a crashing real estate market, sellers are the new bankers for real estate investors.

The passage of new U.S. federal lending laws restricts easy access to new mortgage financing for all real estate buyers, especially investors. Lenders will want to verify everything about a potential borrower including job stability, monthly income and expenses, credit history, financial strength, and ability to make mortgage payments.

If you have a down payment and you have to obtain a new loan from a bank for the balance of the purchase price, unless you have perfect credit, you will not get financing. Investor buyers will have to have cash or look to the seller as banker in order to finance their real estate deals.

## Success Buying or Selling

Your real estate investing success in a crashing real estate market will be determined by two factors. Buying successfully is the first factor. We call this Win Going In. Selling successfully is the second factor. We call this No Doubt Getting Out.

## Win Going In

Again, without perfect credit, the only loans available to investors will be offered by sellers. We will show you how to negotiate with the seller so that the seller will jump at the opportunity to be the banker and sell you his property. You will Win Going In because you have negotiated the right price *and* the right terms. By buying for the right price and the right terms, you can make money when you sell.

## No Doubt Getting Out

You will have No Doubt Getting Out because when you sell, you will sell for the right terms *and* the right price. By employing seller as banker financing when you sell you will generate cash and positive cash flow carrying the mortgage for your buyers.

## Auctioning Your Property for Top Dollar

We show you how to auction your property for top dollar. By using an auction you will receive the highest price possible in a crashing market. We are not talking about a foreclosure auction where the opening bid starts low and you hope buyers bid up the price. We are talking about a version of a Dutch auction where the opening bid starts high and whoever makes the first bid below the opening bid gets the property.

## A New Technique

We present a new technique that successful real estate investors can add to their repertoire to make money investing in a crashing market. This technique is Buy Low and Sell Lower. Using our experience buying and selling we answer two important questions. How does this technique work? How do you make money using this technique?

## Cash and Cash Flow Is King

In normal real estate markets cash is king. This means that if you can pay cash for real estate you typically can get a lower price and therefore a better buy.

## Example

Let's look at an example. A seller is asking $1,000,000 for his New York City condo. In a normal real estate market you, as the buyer, would be concerned with how are you going to come up with the $1,000,000 asking price. If you had $900,000 to $950,000 in cash, you could negotiate a good price with the seller. In a crashing market, the seller may accept $900,000 or less if you have cash.

**Cash Price Savings**

| | |
|---|---:|
| Asking price | $1,000,000 |
| Cash price | −$ 900,000 |
| Cash price savings | $ 100,000 |

In a crashing real estate market cash and cash flow is king. You must create cash and positive cash flow on every one of your deals. Otherwise you will go broke. We show you how to make a profit, create a positive cash flow, and stay in the game as a successful real estate investor.

*The All-New Real Estate Foreclosure, Short-Selling, Underwater, Property Auction, Positive Cash Flow Book* is the only book that shows you how to start with little or no knowledge about investing in real estate and jump in and make money in a crashing market. While everyone else is standing on the sidelines afraid to act, you will be winning the real estate investing game.

When we developed and produced the Foreclosure Training for Robert Allen, our students in Baltimore and Los Angeles were able to put into practice our insider knowledge and make money investing in foreclosures immediately. With *The All-New Real Estate Foreclosure, Short-Selling, Underwater, Property Auction, Positive Cash Flow Book*, you will be able to do what our students did coast to coast and beyond.

# INTRODUCTION

Over the years, we have traveled throughout the world teaching various financial, real estate, success, and trust educational programs through Howell Carey International University (HCIU). We are always striving to be on the leading edge for ourselves and our students. Our investor, brokerage, trustee, and educators experience in the real estate industry lets us give you the practical knowledge and know-how we have acquired to apply to your real estate investing.

Regarding real estate education, we have taught everything from buying and selling it creatively as an individual or investor to core classes for licensing and passing real estate broker's exams. Recently we have co-authored a university course book on real estate principles and a book directed at real estate agents helping them work professionally with buyers and investors.

We have written four books currently available that we recommend you read to give you a broader background and more in-depth training to be more effective in your real estate investing in this crashing market. These include *Quick Cash in Foreclosures* (2004), *Make Money in Real Estate Tax Liens* (2005), *Make Money in Short-Sale Foreclosures* (2006), and *Make Money in Abandoned Properties* (2006). These books are all published by John Wiley & Sons. If you feel like a total newbie and have no money at all you could study and profit from our book *New Path to Real Estate Wealth, Earning Without Owning* (2003). To further help you sell your properties we have a best seller currently available from John Wiley & Sons: *How To Sell Your Home Without a Broker, Fourth Edition* (2004).

## Our Philosophy

Our philosophy has always been that you need to be in control of your investments. Counting on a stock broker, investment adviser, accountant, general partner, or real estate investment fund leaves you completely out of control. When you are an actively engaged real estate investor, you are the one calling the shots. You are the one responsible for your successes and failures.

As we are writing this introduction, the Bernie Madoff Ponzi scheme has unraveled and is in the process of destroying many people's lives. We promise you that you are the only person who can make you rich. Conversely, we promise you that you are the only person who can make you poor. Our mission is to provide you with the knowledge and information you need to be successful. And, if needed, we make ourselves available to you through our university HCIU or with fee-based consulting and partnering if you need that extra knowledge, push, information, or assistance.

## Investing in Real Estate = High Net Worth

Investing in real estate is still the best vehicle to use to amass a high net worth. Do not be paralyzed into investment inaction by the negative media ranting that real estate is no longer a smart investment. Real estate has always been and always will be the small investor's surest way to become a multimillionaire.

The Peruvian-born economist Hernando de Soto got it right when he said the West became the economic world leader when our property laws and banking system gave us the ability to turn illiquid real estate (land) into liquid money. Cash and now cash and cash flow is king of the world. This book will show you how to become king or queen of your financial world.

## How to Read This Book

We recommend you read this book in a particular way. Bring a lot of energy to your reading. This does not mean that you must necessarily read the book quickly, though that is fine with us. We want you to be excited about the material. Highlighters can be your best friend. Highlight items as you go. You could even color code your highlighting. Whatever it takes to enjoy and capture the information we are sharing with you. We want you to Win Going In as you read.

If you find yourself bogging down, stop reading. The material is designed to be comprehended in bursts. See if you can go from one insight to the next. You will become energized when you do this.

We would like to hear from you about your successes. Also, we want to hear what is working and what is not working for you. Please e-mail us at thetrustee@hotmail.com or contact us through our publisher, John Wiley & Sons.

We are available to partner with you on deals that you bring to us. We are available to help you put your deals together for a fee. If we do a partnership with you, we are jointly responsible for its success. If we consult with you on one of your deals, you are responsible for your success. Remember we have thousands of investors wanting to do business with us and thousands of students wanting to receive further education from us so please be patient and our staff will get you to us as soon as possible. When you e-mail please put the target date and topic in the subject line to assist us in sorting time priorities. Remember to include all your contact information and as much detail of the project as possible to expedite our response. Good luck and good deals!

—Chantal and Bill Carey

# THE ALL-NEW REAL ESTATE FORECLOSURE SHORT-SELLING UNDERWATER PROPERTY AUCTION POSITIVE CASH FLOW BOOK

# PART ONE

# The Real Estate Market Has Crashed

Pick a city in the United States: Boston, New York, Atlanta, Miami, Dallas, Chicago, Denver, Los Vegas, Phoenix, San Diego, Los Angeles, San Francisco, Portland, or Seattle. Everywhere in the country the real estate market is crashing—just as it is in other regions around the world. Prices in all 20 major metropolitan areas in the United States measured by the S&P/Case-Shiller Home Price Index are spiraling downward. Nationwide the index plunged 19.1 percent in the last year.

In 2008, in the United States alone, 3,000,000 homeowners received foreclosure filings on their homes. This represents 1 in 54 homes in the United States. According to a national foreclosure list company, more than 860,000 properties were repossessed by lenders last year. Many hundreds of thousands more were bought by real estate investors through short-sales or at the foreclosure auction. In the first six weeks of 2009, foreclosure proceedings began on another 296,000 homeowners according to the Center for Responsible Lending (a nonprofit organization focused on eradicating predatory lending practices).

At least 10 to 12 million households are facing foreclosure over the next four years. In the current economic downturn, 7 million to 8 million people could lose their jobs. They will not be able to make their mortgage payments. January 2009 foreclosure filings were up 18 percent from January 2008. Again, according to a national foreclosure list company 1 in every 466 households nationally received a foreclosure notice in January 2009.

Moody's Economy.com says that 13.8 million of the 52 million United States homeowners with a mortgage (27 percent) owe more on their mortgages than their homes are worth. This is what is known as being *underwater* with your mortgage.

Bank repossession rose 184 percent year-over-year. According to the National Association of Realtors (NAR) in the United States, 19 percent of the inventory of existing homes for sale in January 2009 was bank real estate-owned (REO) properties. This creates a huge downward pull on real estate prices. The median price of a single-family home in the United States was $175,400 in December 2008 down 15.3 percent from a year ago. What happened to the housing boom?

## Financial Derivatives Have Crashed the Real Estate Market

Financial derivatives have crashed the real estate market worldwide. A financial derivative is a contract between a buyer and a seller that derives value based on an underlying asset like a stock or a real estate mortgage. Poor quality mortgages were the underlying assets for trillions of dollars in high-cost derivatives. How did this happen?

A poor quality mortgage occurs when a borrower stops making monthly payments. Media attention has been focused on the subprime mortgage borrower. These were borrowers who were not qualified for A paper or prime mortgage loans. Banks loaned them money based on these borrowers' ability to breathe on a mirror and fog it up. These loans could be characterized as B, C, or D paper.

However, many borrowers of A paper and Alternative A (Alt A) paper have stopped making their mortgage payments, too. Alt A mortgages were given to borrowers who may have had good credit but had no long-term ability to make monthly mortgage payments. These were a version of NINJA loans. A NINJA loan means No Income, No Job, and (No) Assets.

## Adjustable Rate Mortgages

Many A paper and Alternative A (Alt A) paper borrowers' inability to continue making monthly mortgage payments were exacerbated when the mortgage came with an adjustable interest rate and/or adjustable monthly payment. After the initial teaser rate with its correspondingly low payment changed with the first rate adjustment triggering higher monthly payments, these borrowers could not afford to make their monthly mortgage payments.

Added to this banking debacle was the normal cyclical nature of the real estate market. Just as the top of the real estate cycle was being hit and a normal price leveling or price decline was occurring, the rates and payments on millions of real estate loans were adjusting upward.

## Savings and Loan Crisis

In the 1980s, the United States experienced a crisis in the savings and loan industry. Cheap credit, nonexistent lending standards, and weak government regulation caused hundreds of savings and loan institutions to fail. Today, we have those same three factors at work plus two new ones.

The first new factor is that banking is no longer local. Banking is now global. Look what happened to the country of Iceland when its banks went under. The government collapsed. The second new factor is the packaging of mortgage debt into securities (derivatives) beyond the control of any government regulation.

From 1995 to 2005, Bank of America, JPMorgan Chase, and Citigroup became international players buying and selling stocks and bonds and managing assets such as mortgage-backed securities for big fees. This has been referred to as the universal bank model.

## Acting Locally and Globally

These big banks were acting locally and globally. From 1995 to 2008, bank branches in the United States went from 81,000 to 99,000. This was a 22 percent increase. First-time home buyers and people wanting to pull equity out of their homes were encouraged to come in and borrow money. Unscrupulous mortgage brokers aggressively pursued predatory lending practices in order to maximize their profits.

In one of the most egregious cases of predatory lending practices discovered so far, Ray Vargas of Cerritos, California, was hit with unconscionable lending fess, prepayment penalties, and interest charges. An investigation by msnbc.com showed that in a "21-month period in 2005 and 2006, Vargas' home was refinanced five times through a total of six loans."

According to msnbc.com his loan total went from $213,555 to $745,000. To access this $531,445 in equity Mr. Vargas "paid at least $123,237 in loan origination fess and prepayment penalties," according to the report. He paid another $60,000 in interest. This occurred as he was coping with the death of his wife of 57 years and her huge medical and nursing home bills. By the way, Mr. Vargas is 84. So what did the banks do with all these new loans?

### *Bundling*

The banks then bundled together trillions of dollars of these mortgages and sold them to investors all around the world. Mortgages on properties in California, Nevada, Florida, or Rhode Island would become the underlying assets to financial derivatives sold to hedge funds in Paris, London, Singapore, or Shanghai.

In the past, credit had been extended based on the borrower's ability to repay the loan. Now credit was being extended based on the lender's ability to package a mortgage loan as a security instrument and sell it. Mortgage borrowers like Ray Vargas were just a means to an end. The big investment banks like Lehman Brothers, Merrill Lynch, Morgan Stanley, and Goldman Sachs saw how much money was being made and jumped into the game.

## Wall Street Took over Main Street

Wall Street took over Main Street. These firms bought and sold mortgage-backed securities by borrowing astronomical amounts of money. In 2006, Goldman Sachs made a $9.4 billion profit, which was the highest in Wall Street history. Morgan Stanley made a profit of $7.1 billion. Their respective CEOs were paid bonuses of $53.4 million and $41.4 million.

Then toward the end of 2006 the housing market began to cool off. Subprime loans were the first to implode. This was the beginning of the end. During 2007 and 2008, all the players involved experienced massive losses, as many borrowers in all types of mortgage categories stopped making their mortgage payments for various reasons. Banks now have $5 trillion in nonperforming assets (potential losses) crushing their balance sheets.

# AIG (American International Group)

AIG made a fortune selling insurance contracts to banks and hedge funds guaranteeing the value of the derivative contracts. By the fall of 2008, the United States Federal Reserve made the decision to rescue AIG. One hundred and fifty billion dollars later and the company that we have been told is too big to be allowed to fail is still failing. Without the government rescue the whole banking system would have collapsed under the domino effect because no bank's assets were worth the paper they were written on.

One portfolio of AIG assets the Federal Reserve holds is valued at $20 billion of residential mortgage-backed securities. A second portfolio is valued at $27 billion and consists of collateralized debt obligations, which are financial derivatives that combine slices of debt. These investment portfolios are made up of billions of dollars of toxic paper. Sorting out the toxic paper from the nontoxic paper is just one of the problems.

# Financial Derivatives Are the Solution

However, noted expert and professor of economics at Yale University, Robert Shiller believes that financial derivatives are the solution to the current financial crisis. Financial derivatives are a risk management tool according to Shiller. He equates them to an insurance policy. "You pay a premium and if an event happens, you get a payment," says Shiller.

Robert Shiller is the Shiller of the S&P/Case-Shiller Home Price Index. Movement in this index can be traded on the Chicago Mercantile Exchange.

Shiller wants homeowners and lenders to be able to insure themselves against falling housing prices. He proposes doing this by using a version of a financial derivative. Let's look at an example.

## Example

You buy a home for $350,000. You make a 20 percent down payment of $70,000. You borrow $280,000 from your mortgage lender.

### Home Purchase

| | |
|---|---|
| Purchase price | $350,000 |
| Down payment | − $ 70,000 |
| Mortgage amount | $280,000 |

You buy a derivative that is inversely related to the nearest regional S&P/Case-Shiller Home Price Index to your property. If the value of your property drops and by extension the Home Price Index drops, the financial derivative would go up in value and offset your loss.

Let's say the value of your home drops 30 percent or $105,000 because of changing market conditions. Now your home is worth $245,000.

### Home Value Drops

| | |
|---|---|
| Property value | $350,000 |
| Loss in value | −$105,000 |
| New property value | $245,000 |

You are effectively underwater with your mortgage of $280,000 being $35,000 greater than the value of your property.

### Underwater

| | |
|---|---|
| Mortgage amount | $280,000 |
| New property value | −$245,000 |
| Underwater | $ 35,000 |

Your financial derivative would go up in value from 0 to $105,000. This would recoup your $70,000 down payment and your $35,000 underwater amount.

### Derivative Value

| | |
|---|---|
| Down payment | $ 70,000 |
| Underwater amount | +$ 35,000 |
| Derivative value | $105,000 |

## Lenders Use Derivatives Locally not Globally

Lenders could do the same thing as their borrowers. By buying a derivative, the lender would have a hedge against having to foreclose and likely winding up owning property the lender is not interested in owning. If a borrower stopped paying on a mortgage loan the derivative would cure the deficiency.

It would also protect the lender from having to do a short-sale. A short-sale would require the lender to cram down the loan amount from $280,000 to $245,000 in order for the property to sell at the current market value. This would result in at least a $35,000 loss to the lender.

### Lender Loss

| | |
|---|---|
| Mortgage amount | $280,000 |
| Cram down amount | −$245,000 |
| Lender loss | $ 35,000 |

## $20 Trillion Housing Market

By having derivatives available for borrowers and lenders, the $20 trillion housing market can become more liquid. Without derivatives there are very limited ways to unlock profit when the market falls. The stock market allows options and derivatives. This allows money to be made even when the market is falling.

This significantly increases the number of buyers and sellers in the stock market. More buyers and more sellers mean more liquidity. More liquidity means a better functioning market even in turbulent conditions.

## History

In the 1920s, U.S. mortgage lending was a very simple financial transaction. If you wanted to borrow money to buy a home you went to your local bank. The bank gave you the money to buy your home and you gave the bank a promissory note and a mortgage contract.

The promissory note was the evidence of your debt to your bank. The mortgage contract was the security device that gave the bank the legal right to foreclose on your ownership title in the event you defaulted on your monthly payments.

The bank got the money to loan to you by borrowing it from all the depositors who put money in the bank. In return for putting money in the bank, the bank gave each depositor a passbook showing how much money they had on deposit. The bank also paid a small amount of interest to encourage people to take their money out of their coffee cans and mattresses and bring it to the bank.

The banks made money on the interest rate spread between what they were paying their depositors and what they were being paid by their mortgage borrowers. If a bank was paying 1 percent to its depositors and receiving 4 percent from its mortgage borrowers, the interest rate spread was 3 percent. This is what is known as the primary mortgage market.

## Primary Mortgage Market

The primary mortgage market is a financial transaction between the bank and a mortgage borrower. The money went from the bank to the borrower. The promissory note and mortgage contract went from the borrower to the bank.

### Primary Mortgage Market

Money →

Bank                                        Borrower

← Paper

In other words, the money went in one direction and the paper went in the other direction. This system worked well until the stock market in the United States crashed and the depression of the 1930s ensued.

## Recession, Depression, Panic

Let's be clear. Today we talk about a contraction of the economy as a recession. The word is not even capitalized so as to downplay what is really going on in the economy. A recession is defined as two consecutive quarters of negative economic growth as measured by the gross domestic product (GDP).

Recessions used to be called depressions. However, politically the word depression is too unpalatable a term. So in the modern era we have sugarcoated economic difficulty with a word that sounds like something you looked forward to in grade school: recess-ion.

The United States in the 1870s had banking panics. By the 1930s the political powers that be substituted the word depression for panic. Talking about an economic depression had a much milder emotional impact than talking about an economic panic. It also allowed politicians to get reelected.

## Crisis of Confidence

The reality of the 1930s was another banking panic. People wanted the banks to give them back their cash when the economy got into trouble. All the depositors showed up at the same time and said, "Here is my passbook. Give me my money." But the banks could not comply.

The banks had loaned out the money for people to buy real estate. The banks had very little cash because they were holding the mortgage papers. This is called a run on the bank. Thousands of banks failed. Millions of Americans lost all their money.

## History Repeats Itself

History is now repeating itself. According to RBC Capital Markets, 1,000 banks will fail in 2009 and 2010. In July 2008, we had the run on IndyMac Bank. This was a national banking conglomerate with $32 billion of assets. Unfortunately, many billions of these assets were toxic. The bank was rocked by losses on defaulted mortgages made at the top of the housing boom.

In September 2008, Washington Mutual was seized by the United States government. Over a 10-day period $16.4 billion in deposits was withdrawn from the bank by panicked customers. Before it collapsed Washington Mutual was the sixth largest bank in the country. It held more than $327 billion in assets. This was 10 times the amount of assets held by IndyMac Bank. It was the largest bank failure ever. Perhaps we should say so far.

## Fannie Mae

In response to the collapse of the primary mortgage market in the 1930s because of the lack of liquidity in the system, the United States federal government created the Federal National Mortgage Association or Fannie Mae in 1938. The purpose of Fannie Mae was to create a secondary mortgage market and prevent banking panics.

### *Secondary Mortgage Market*

The mortgage paper would be passed from the bank to Fannie Mae. In return, Fannie Mae would send money to the bank. That way, when the depositors showed up with their passbooks and said, "Give me my money," the bank actually had the cash to give them.

### Secondary Mortgage Market

Money→

Fannie Mae                                    Bank

← Paper

The bank went from being the owner of the mortgage paper to being the servicing agent for Fannie Mae and receiving a fee for collecting the mortgage payments from the borrower.

The secondary mortgage market system was expanded in 1968 and again in 1970. In 1968, Fannie Mae acquired a sister, Ginnie Mae, the Government National Mortgage Association. The Federal Home Loan Mortgage Corporation, Freddie Mac, was added in 1970.

What most people do not know is that Fannie Mae was privatized in 1968 to remove its activities from the federal budget. Freddie Mac has been privately owned since its inception. Even though they both had the word federal in their names, neither company was federal until the federal government took them over in the last quarter of 2008. Now they are both "federalized."

## Today

Today there are $10.5 trillion in mortgages in the United States according to the Federal Reserve. More than 90 percent of these mortgages are now owned by someone other than the bank that made the loan in the primary mortgage market.

Fannie Mae and Freddie Mac got into trouble because they packaged and sold mortgage-backed securities. Fannie and Freddie wanted more liquidity and profits so they created a tertiary mortgage market. They sold the mortgage-backed securities to hedge funds in return for big cash profits.

### Tertiary Mortgage Market

Money→

Hedge funds                          Fannie/Freddie

←Paper

This tertiary mortgage market was a global market. It was a giant Ponzi scheme played out on the global stage in trillions of dollars. As long as everyone was making big fees packaging and servicing these securities, then everything was hunky-dory-copasetic-peachy-keen.

In fact, it was impossible to determine the value of the securities Fannie Mae and Freddie Mac were selling. That is still the problem today. No one can figure out how to separate the toxic securities from the nontoxic securities.

Once the housing market cooled in the United States and people stopped making payments on their mortgages, the cash flow that drove this whole system dried up. One part of the United States government bailout was the immediate cash infusion of $66 billion in combined subsidies to Fannie Mae and Freddie Mac.

## The Impasse

So far the solution to this mortgage mess has remained at an impasse. The impasse was described quite succinctly by Steve Preston, a former housing secretary in the Bush administration:

> *We still have somewhat of an impasse between the people who are sending you your mortgage bills, your (loan) servicers, and people who own your mortgages. That's an impasse we have to break."*

(Feb. 10, 2009)

The loan servicing companies act as the go-between to collect payments from homeowners and distribute them to investors. They have behaved with tortoise-like speed to loan modification requests from homeowners. Their position is based on the liability they have to investors like Fannie Mae and Freddie Mac should they modify a loan without these investors' approval; they are afraid of being sued by these investors.

### Hope for Homeowners

The United States Congress passed the Hope for Homeowners program, which was to run from October 1, 2008 to September 30, 2011. The goal of the program was to help at least 400,000 homeowners modify or refinance their potentially foreclosure-causing adjustable rate mortgages into 30-year fixed-rate loans. This program has been an abysmal failure. Unrealistic restrictions and exorbitantly high fees allowed only 25 homeowners to be approved by the end of 2008.

## New Programs

Under a new program created by Federal Deposit Insurance Corporation (FDIC), guidelines were developed to accelerate the modification of mortgages held by the failed IndyMac Bank. This program would provide financial incentives to loan servicers to modify loans and give them legal protection from investor lawsuits if they follow certain guidelines. This program became the template adopted by the Obama administration to rescue the real estate market.

## Homeowner Stability Initiative

The Obama administration wants to stop the 10 million to 12 million foreclosures that are projected to happen over the first and what would be the only four-year term for President Obama if nothing is done. The Obama plan would keep 4 to 5 million homeowners in their homes.

Under the Homeowner Stability Initiative, the government would invest $75 billion to buy millions of mortgages that are in default or are about to go into default. Rather than paying par value, the mortgages would be bought at a discount.

Using our example from earlier in the chapter, the government would buy the $280,000 mortgage for the current market value of the property or no more than $245,000. This $35,000 cram down is a 12.5 percent discount.

### Cram Down Percentage

$$\frac{\$35,000}{\$280,000} = 12.5$$

Of course, the government may want a bigger discount and force the lender to accept a bigger cram down on the loan payoff.

### *Refinance*

The Homeowner Stability Initiative would then allow the homeowner to refinance the new loan amount at a lower interest rate and for a lower monthly payment thus preventing the homeowner from falling into foreclosure.

With the Treasury injecting another $200 billion into Fannie Mae and Freddie Mac, the secondary mortgage market would be revived. Mortgage lenders making new loans or refinancing existing loans would be able to pass the mortgage paper to Fannie Mae or Freddie Mac and receive the cash back to make more loans.

## Two Questions

You should have at least two questions at this point. Your first question should be: "How can I feel comfortable investing in this crashing real estate market?" Your second question should be, assuming you decide to get involved: "How do I make money investing in a crashing real estate market?"

To answer your first question: We have just told you the U.S. federal government is going to get involved to the tune of at least $275 billion in this crashing real estate market. It is always a good thing to have substantial money partners involved in the market with you. That bodes well for the long-term health of the market.

The answer to the second question is what the rest of this book is about. Before you can make money investing in a crashing real estate market you have to have a strategy. In the next chapter we will talk about building a quick cash *and* a long-term wealth-building strategy.

# CHAPTER 2

# Make Money Investing in a Crashed Real Estate Market

To make money investing in a crashing real estate market you must first develop a strategy. Two strategies to make money investing in a crashing real estate market are *quick cash* and *long-term wealth building*. Rather than choosing one or the other of these strategies we recommend you use both. We suggest you use a quick cash *and* a long-term wealth building strategy.

Some real estate investors employ the real estate investment strategy of long-term wealth building. In long-term wealth building you buy and hold property for income and appreciation. This can be a very effective strategy in areas of the country that historically have experienced very high rates of price appreciation such as California and the Northeast.

However, once you invest your money in real estate, it can be difficult to liquidate or sell your real estate assets quickly. Since real estate is the biggest ticket item for most people, there are the fewest buyers in the marketplace compared to most other commodities. The quick cash strategy addresses the key problem historically associated with real estate investing: the lack of liquidity.

## Quick Cash Strategy

If you want to keep yourself more liquid in your investments, we recommend you use a quick cash strategy to make money investing in a crashing real estate market. Another name for the quick cash strategy is *flipping*. Flipping is the fastest way to make money in real estate. When you flip a property you get in and out of the investment in a short period of time.

Investing in real estate can be very cash intensive. For example, when you buy a foreclosure on the courthouse steps, you have to pay cash. Usually there are renovation expenses with foreclosures that require cash outlays.

Also, there may be holding costs like hazard insurance, property taxes, homeowner's association fees, and mortgage payments if you get new financing. You may have to flip your foreclosure property so you can get your cash out in order to be able to buy another foreclosure deal.

## Top 10 Advantages of the Quick Cash Strategy

The quick cash strategy is especially useful for foreclosure investing. We like quick cash because we don't like being landlords (we've tried it), we love the art of the deal (flipping allows you to make lots of deals), and we like making money right away. Here are the top 10 advantages of using the quick cash strategy.

### Number 10: No Income Tax Problems

One of the major advantages of the quick cash strategy is that you avoid income tax problems. When you hold rental real estate it is very easy to recapture depreciation when you sell the property. Current tax law has you paying a 25 percent tax when you recapture depreciation. How easy is it to recapture depreciation? Just own rental real estate and take depreciation. When you sell the property you will recapture the depreciation.

### Number 9: No Extensive Record Keeping

When you own rental real estate you must keep extensive records. You will either have a full-time job as a bookkeeper or you will be paying a bookkeeper.

You will have rent receipts, security deposit receipts, and checkbooks (notice we used the plural here). You will have checking accounts to reconcile. How about the legal requirement in some areas of having a trust account for tenant security deposits?

You will keep maintenance records. You may have employees with all the paperwork and tax nightmares that entails. You will have to deal with items such as workers' compensation insurance, unemployment insurance, health insurance, Occupational Safety and Health Administration (OSHA) regulation compliance, Social Security taxes, and federal income tax withholding. The list goes on and on.

### Number 8: No Lawsuits

If you own real property, there is a very high probability that you will be sued. You will be sued by one of your tenants, their guests, or by a cutthroat attorney. This is the type of attorney who looks up your real estate holdings in the public record to determine whether they will take a case based on the value of the real estate assets you own that they can go after.

When you own property you become a target for frivolous lawsuits. Some of you reading this know exactly what we are talking about because you have been sued for no apparent reason. We also know that some of you have paid legal settlements just to make the frivolous lawsuits go away.

What is our solution? Don't own real property. Not even foreclosure property. The secret is to *control* real property, not own real property. That is what the quick cash strategy is all about.

### Number 7: No Homeowner's Association

If you are, or have ever been, part of a homeowner's association, you know the frustration of dealing with mini tyrants. Not to mention the $100, $200, or $300 monthly dues.

And what about the special assessments for painting, landscaping, or roofing that can run into the thousands of dollars? And, if you don't pay your monthly dues or special assessments, your friendly homeowner's association can foreclose on you and/or sue you.

Homeowner's associations are no longer just attached to condominiums or townhouses. We are seeing an increasing number of "maintenance associations" attached to Planned Unit Developments (PUDs) and single-family residences (houses).

### Number 6: No Repairs, Maintenance, or Capital Improvements Costs

We are sure you have heard the expression "deferred maintenance." Deferred maintenance is the polite way of saying a property is a fixer-upper. Usually this is because the property owner did not spend any money on regular maintenance through the years. When a property is in foreclosure you can bet the last thing the property owner will spend money on is repairs, maintenance, and capital improvements.

Real estate ownership entails significant repairs, maintenance, and capital improvements costs. A plumbing repair may cost $275. Lawn and pool maintenance may be several hundreds of dollars a month. What if the property needs a new roof for $7,500 or a new dishwasher for $400? Using a quick cash strategy helps you avoid these costs.

#### Repairs, Maintenance, and Capital Improvements Costs

| | |
|---|---:|
| Plumbing repair | $  275 |
| Lawn & pool maintenance | 325 |
| New roof | 7,500 |
| New dishwasher | + 400 |
| Total costs | $8,500 |

And this is just your first month's outlay!

### Number 5: No Hazard Insurance

No fire insurance, liability insurance, or earthquake insurance. No insurance, period. The last time we checked, any kind of hazard insurance is expensive. And real estate lenders calculate a monthly insurance payment when qualifying you for a real estate loan, even when you prepay the insurance premium in an escrow account for the next year.

### Number 4: No Property Taxes

Depending on your local regulations you may pay property taxes once a year or perhaps twice a year. In places like Texas where there is no state income tax, property taxes can be quite substantial on even modest properties.

For example, on a property valued at $161,000 by the county tax assessor for a particular area in Texas, the annual property tax bill can amount to $5,000! If you calculate that on a monthly basis you are paying over $400 a month for every month you own the property.

### Monthly Property Taxes

| | |
|---|---|
| Annual property taxes | $5,000.00 |
| Divided by 12 months | 12 |
| Monthly property taxes | = $   417 |

## Number 3: No Monthly Mortgage Payments

Do you want month in and month out, 12 months a year for 30 years to make a mortgage payment? That is 360 payments. Let's look at an example. A $315,000 loan for 30 years at 6 percent interest is payable at $1,888.58 monthly including principal and interest. Multiply the monthly payment by 360 payments and you will pay a total of $679,980.30.

### Monthly Payments

| | |
|---|---|
| Monthly payment | $   1,888.58 |
| 30 years $\times$ 12  = | $\times$ 360 |
| Total of payments | $679,890.30 |

The really nauseating number is when you realize that you originally borrowed $315,000! You wind up paying $364,890.30 in interest.

### Amount of Interest

| | |
|---|---|
| Total of payments | $679,890.30 |
| Amount borrowed | −315,000.00 |
| Amount of interest | $364,890.30 |

That is 116 percent of the amount you borrowed.

### Percent of Amount Borrowed

| | |
|---|---|
| Amount of interest | $364,890.30 |
| Amount borrowed | $315,000.00 |
| % of amount borrowed | =  116% |

## Number 2: No Landlord Role

There are quite a number of horror stories out there related to being a landlord. Do you really think you can be a successful landlord? Being a landlord is a heartless, thankless job. No matter what you do, you are wrong.

If you are too nice, the tenants will take advantage of your concern for them and leave you with uncollectible rent when you finally get them to move out. If you take a strictly business approach, the tenants will complain to the powers-that-be that you are a heartless money-grubber and leave you with uncollectible rent when you finally evict them.

**The History of Landlords**   Being a lord or a lady of the land has a noble heritage. In olden times there was a symbiotic relationship between the lords and ladies and their tenants. The tenants lived on the lords' and ladies' property, raised their families, and farmed the land.

In return, the tenants paid rent to the lords and ladies in the form of most of the crops they grew. There was no money. Or rather, most people, like the tenants, did not have money because there were no jobs. Everyone's job was working the land.

Unfortunately, this romantic symbiotic relationship from the Middle Ages has been shattered by the realities of today's world. As a landlord you are a target for other people's problems. Keep that in mind as you acquire rental property.

## Number 1: Quick Cash

And the number one advantage of the quick cash strategy is quick cash. Cash is king! Long live the king! The problem with real estate investing for most people is that it takes far too long to make any money. Yes, we know that if you bought a two-bedroom, one-bathroom home in Anywhere, California, in 1968 for $20,000 like our friend John did, you would be sitting on a property worth $1,000,000 today. But who has the time, or the patience to wait? We don't, do you?

Flipping is your answer. When you are a real estate investor whose strategy is quick cash, patience does not have to be one of your strengths. In fact, being impatient becomes one of your strengths! You become impatient with the deal you are working on and want to get it done so you can get on to the next deal. The more deals you get involved with, the more money you will make.

## Long-Term Wealth Building Strategy

We know some of you will prefer using a long-term wealth building strategy to make money investing in a crashing real estate market. Another way to describe the long-term wealth building strategy is buying and holding property for income and appreciation. In a crashing real estate market we recommend you employ both quick cash *and* long-term wealth building strategies.

## Top 10 Advantages of Long-Term Wealth Building

We are going to give you the top 10 advantages of using the long-term wealth building strategy. The long-term wealth building strategy is also useful for foreclosure investing. While you may prefer the quick cash strategy, there may be times you will want to buy and hold your foreclosure properties. This decision may depend upon in what area of the world you are making your investments.

### Number 10: Depreciation

There may be income tax advantages for real estate investors who materially participate in the management of their rental properties. You may be able to take depreciation on the improvements and use this depreciation to offset the income the property produces.

Let's say you receive $1,300 in monthly rent for 12 months. This is $15,600 in yearly income. If you are able to take $10,000 in annual depreciation, then you will only have to pay taxes on $5,600 in annual income.

### Taxable Rental Income

| | |
|---|---|
| Annual income | $15,600 |
| Annual depreciation | $-10,000$ |
| Taxable income | $ 5,600 |

### Number 9: Rehabbing

Rehabbing can be an important component in the value of a property. Real estate investors who rehab a foreclosure property contribute not only to their own bottom line, but also to the value of the surrounding community.

A property that is rehabbed generates two to three dollars for every dollar spent rehabbing when you sell the property down the road if you do it right. If you put $20,000 into rehabbing a property suitably you can usually count on a $40,000 to $60,000 value increase as long as you stay within market values for the area in which the property is located.

### Rehab Profit

| | |
|---|---|
| Rehab amount | <$20,000> |
| Value increase | +60,000 |
| Rehab profit | $40,000 |

## Number 8: Deductibility of Property Taxes

All of the property taxes you pay on the property may be tax deductible. When you pay the property taxes you may be able to use this to offset the income the property produces.

Let's say you receive $1,300 in monthly rent for 12 months. This translates into $15,600 in annual income. If you pay $5,000 in property taxes, you will only have to pay tax on $10,600 in annual income.

### Property Tax Deductiblity

| | |
|---|---|
| Annual income | $15,600 |
| Property taxes | −5,000 |
| Taxable income | $10,600 |

## Number 7: Deductibility of Mortgage Interest

All of the mortgage interest you pay on the mortgages you used to purchase the property may be tax deductible. You may be able to use the mortgage interest you pay to offset the income the property produces.

Let's say you receive $1,300 in monthly rent for 12 months. This is $15,600 in annual income. If you pay $8,000 in mortgage interest, then you will only have to pay tax on $7,600 in annual income.

### Mortgage Interest Deductibility

| | |
|---|---|
| Annual income | $15,600 |
| Mortgage interest | −8,000 |
| Taxable income | $ 7,600 |

If we put depreciation, property tax, and mortgage interest deductibility together from our examples we would have $10,000, $5,000, and $8,000, respectively. This totals $23,000.

### Total Deduction

| | |
|---|---|
| Annual depreciation | $10,000 |
| Property taxes | 5,000 |
| Mortgage interest | +8,000 |
| Total deduction | $23,000 |

This easily offsets our $15,600 in rental income. In fact, the $7,400 excess deduction may be used to offset other income. Check with your tax adviser.

### Excess Deduction

| | |
|---|---|
| Yearly income | $15,600 |
| Total deduction | <23,000> |
| xcess deduction | <$ 7,400> |

## Number 6: Long-Term Capital Gains

You may receive long-term capital gains tax treatment for property held over one year. This can be a huge tax savings compared with being taxed at ordinary income tax rates. Comparing an ordinary income tax rate of 28 percent with a long-term capital gains rate of 15 percent, you can see that you practically cut your tax bill in half.

Let's say you have a profit of $50,000. At a 28 percent ordinary income tax rate you would pay $14,000 in income tax. At a 15 percent long-term capital gains rate you would pay $7,500 in income tax. You save $6,500 in taxes.

### Tax Savings

| | |
|---|---|
| Ordinary income tax rate (28%) | $14,000 |
| Capital gains tax rate (15%) | −7,500 |
| Tax savings | $ 6,500 |

## Number 5: 1031 Tax Deferred Exchanges

You may be able to defer income tax consequences by doing a 1031 tax deferred exchange. Even with favorable long-term capital gains treatment your tax bill can still be quite substantial.

Let's say you have a long-term capital gain of $200,000. At a 15 percent long-term capital gain tax rate your tax bill will be $30,000 if you sell the property.

**Taxes You Owe**

| | |
|---|---|
| Long-term capital gain | $200,000 |
| Long-term capital gains tax rate | × 15% |
| Taxes you owe | $ 30,000 |

By doing a 1031 tax deferred exchange you will defer having the $200,000 long-term gain recognized. Because the gain is not recognized there is no tax consequence to you at the time of the sale. You will have an additional $30,000 in your pocket available to make another real estate investment.

## Number 4: Economies of Scale

A nice advantage of long-term wealth building is being able to capitalize on economies of scale as a landlord. When you have accumulated 5, 10, or 15 properties, you can begin a cookie cutter property management style.

If there is a sale on paint, you buy paint for all your properties. If there is a sale on carpeting or flooring, you buy carpeting or flooring for all your properties. By buying in bulk you save money. It is like buying wholesale instead of retail.

## Number 3: Cash Flow

People who use the long-term wealth building strategy want to build in cash flow for any properties they are going to keep. Cash flow contributes to your overall bottom line. In a crashing real estate market cash flow is king.

When your income exceeds your expenses, you have positive cash flow. This is a good thing. When your expenses exceed your income, you have negative cash flow, which is, of course, a bad thing.

## Number 2: Appreciation

Every real estate market appreciates. In a crashing market it looks like there is no appreciation. However, when considered from a historical perspective real estate has always been a hedge against inflation. Some markets appreciate at a much higher rate than others. Let's take a look at the net differences among these various market appreciation rates.

If you are in a market that appreciates at 4 percent annually your property values will double every 18 years. If you are in a market that appreciates at 7 percent annually your property values will double every 10 years.

Consider what your investment goals are when choosing the market area for your long-term wealth building. Markets that have seen rapid appreciation and are now going down in value will find a floor. Areas like Phoenix, Arizona, will rise again from the ashes of price deflation.

### Number 1: Long-Term Wealth Building

And the number one advantage of the long-term wealth building strategy is long-term wealth building. You are building a future nest egg by using this strategy. By holding property you are compounding your equity year after year without any income tax consequence.

While the quick cash strategy brings you quick cash, unless you are disciplined enough to save or reinvest some of your quick cash, it will disappear as quickly as it appeared.

The future is going to come no matter which investment strategy you choose. That is why we recommend you employ both strategies when investing in a crashing real estate market. You have to decide which property fits into your long-term wealth building portfolio and which property will work best for you for quick cash.

## Best Arena to Make Money

We are now going to turn to the foreclosure arena. Foreclosures are going to be the best arena to make money over the next 48 months. Starting from the basics we will show you how to apply the quick cash and long-term wealth building strategy to your foreclosure investing.

For those of you who are knowledgeable about foreclosures you may want to go to Chapter 4: The New Foreclosure Strategy. For those of you who are new to the foreclosure game we recommend you read straight through the book continuing on with Chapter 3: Foreclosures, Foreclosures, and Foreclosures.

# Foreclosures, Foreclosures, and Foreclosures

The economy and the real estate market are cyclical. Foreclosures are one of the areas in real estate that you can be successful when there is a down market. There is a lot of money to be made in the real estate foreclosure market. First you have to be very knowledgeable about traditional foreclosures. Then you can get involved with short-sale foreclosures.

We are going to spend some time training you in the foreclosure process. There are slight variations on foreclosure procedures from area to area, however, the basic process is the same almost everywhere.

What varies from one area to another is the time period allowed for foreclosure. Do not get too caught up in what may seem to be very technical information. We present this information so you can get a sense of what is involved in a foreclosure. Use this chapter as your foreclosure reference guide.

## Foreclosure

There is no more dreaded word in the real estate world than *foreclosure*. It doesn't matter if you are the real estate borrower or the real estate lender. No one likes to be in a foreclosure situation.

Foreclosure occurs when a real estate lender, whether an institutional real estate lender or a private real estate lender, takes the title to a property away from the borrower in lieu of receiving mortgage payments. Said more formally, when all else has failed, a real estate lender will pursue allowed legal prerogatives to recover the collateral for the real estate loan in order to sell it and recoup the loan proceeds.

The definition of foreclosure is to shut out, exclude, bar, or deprive a person of the right to redeem a mortgage. Foreclosure is not only a process to recover a lender's collateral but also a procedure whereby a borrower's rights of redemption are eliminated and all interests in the subject property are removed.

## Wholesale Real Estate

Foreclosures are by definition wholesale real estate. Why would you want to pay retail for anything that you can buy wholesale? Real estate is no different. When you are buying foreclosures you are buying real estate at a wholesale price. And, since real estate is usually the highest priced commodity that people buy, when you buy real estate wholesale, you have an opportunity to make a lot of money.

From a quick cash strategy point of view, foreclosures give you the opportunity to flip either the property or the real estate contract associated with the property. From a long-term wealth building point of view, foreclosures give you the opportunity to buy real estate wholesale and hold it for income and appreciation.

### *Property Condition*

You might think that foreclosure properties are run down or in poor shape. While this is certainly the case for some of the foreclosure properties that we have been involved with, it is not always the case. You might also think foreclosure properties are in bad neighborhoods. Again, while that can be the case, we have found foreclosures in some very nice neighborhoods that were in very good condition.

## Real Estate Lenders

Ninety-five percent of the foreclosure market begins and ends with real estate lenders. When you understand how lenders operate, you will increase the likelihood of being successful with foreclosure investing.

There are two keys: (1) Lenders get the money they make real estate loans with at a wholesale interest rate; and (2) lenders only make wholesale real estate loans at usually no more than an 80 percent loan to the value of the property.

Let's look at how real estate lenders operate in the real estate market. Real estate lenders make money by loaning money. As we have said lenders get the money to loan from people like you and us.

When people put money in the bank, the bank pays them interest for their money. When the bank loans money to someone to buy real estate, it loans the money at a higher interest rate than the interest it pays to its customers.

## Wholesale Interest

You could say that the bank pays a wholesale interest rate to get its money and then receives a retail interest rate when it loans its money. For example, a bank may pay three percent interest to its customers for certificates of deposit (CDs). Then the bank turns around and loans the money from the certificates of deposit to real estate borrowers for real estate loans at six or seven percent interest.

That is a spread of three or four percentage points. The bank makes money on the spread between the wholesale interest rate it pays on the CDs and the retail interest rate it charges on the real estate loans.

## Wholesale Loans

Real estate lenders will only loan 80 percent of the appraised value of the real estate to protect themselves in the event the borrower defaults on the loan payments. In other words, a real estate lender will only make a wholesale real estate loan. The amount the lender loans is called the loan to value ratio. How much money will a bank loan on a property that has an appraised value of $200,000?

### Loan to Value Ratio

| | |
|---|---|
| Appraised value | $200,000 |
| Maximum loan percentage | × 80% |
| Maximum loan amount | $160,000 |

As you can see from the above numbers, real estate lenders protect themselves by making sure they have a 20 percent cushion between the appraised value, $200,000, and the loan value, $160,000.

### Lender Protection

| | |
|---|---:|
| Appraised value | $200,000 |
| Maximum loan amount | − 160,000 |
| Lender protection | $  40,000 |

## Buyer Default

This $40,000 lender protection is typically the borrower's down payment on the property. Even if the borrower defaults to the tune of $10,000, the lender is protected.

### Lender Protection

| | |
|---|---:|
| Appraised value | $200,000 |
| Maximum loan amount | − 160,000 |
| Lender protection | $  40,000 |
| Default amount | − 10,000 |
| Lender protection | $  30,000 |
| Lender loss | 0 |

## 90 Percent or 95 Percent Loan to Value Ratio

What about real estate lenders who loan 90 percent or 95 percent of the retail value? Won't that put them in jeopardy in the event of a default?

That's where private mortgage insurance (PMI) companies step in. For an insurance premium paid by the borrower, the private mortgage insurer will insure the real estate lender for any defaults above an 80 percent loan to value ratio.

Let's say the borrower received a 90 percent loan from the lender ($180,000) and made only a 10 percent down payment ($20,000) on the same $200,000 property.

### Loan to Value Ratio

| | |
|---|---:|
| Appraised value | $200,000 |
| Loan percentage | × 90% |
| Loan amount | $180,000 |

With the same $10,000 borrower default, the lender still has $10,000 of protection.

## Lender Protection

| | |
|---|---:|
| Appraised value | $200,000 |
| Maximum loan amount | −180,000 |
| Lender protection | $ 20,000 |
| Default amount | −10,000 |
| Lender protection | $ 10,000 |
| Lender loss | 0 |

Even if the borrower defaulted in the amount of $25,000, the private mortgage insurance would pick up the additional $5,000 beyond the borrower's $20,000 equity (down payment). This is another reason why real estate lenders will agree to make short-sale foreclosure deals. The amount of money they may be out beyond the loan amount may be covered by private mortgage insurance.

## Private Mortgage Insurance

| | |
|---|---:|
| Appraised value | $200,000 |
| Maximum loan amount | −180,000 |
| Lender protection | $ 20,000 |
| Default amount | −25,000 |
| Lender protection | ($ 5,000) |
| Private mortgage insurance | $ 5,000 |
| Lender loss | 0 |

Next, let's take a look at the various types of foreclosures.

# Types of Foreclosure

## *Power of Sale Foreclosure*

A power of sale foreclosure is based on the terms of the deed of trust or the mortgage contract, giving the lender, or the trustee, the right to sell the collateral property without being required to spend the time and money involved in a court foreclosure suit. Let's use Texas to illustrate an example of a power of sale foreclosure.

In Texas, these nonjudicial foreclosures are more common than judicial foreclosures (lawsuits in court). The right to exercise the power of sale must be created in writing and is usually part of the deed of trust, which must clearly state that there is a right of nonjudicial foreclosure. The power of sale foreclosure is popular in Texas because it allows the trustee to sell the property more quickly and thus recover the lender's collateral in a timely manner.

The trustee named in the deed of trust has the power to sell the defaulted mortgaged property upon the request of the real estate lender or beneficiary of the trust deed. The trustee must then carefully follow the terms and conditions stated in the deed of trust for the foreclosure. The foreclosure sale must also follow the legal procedures of the state of Texas.

## Texas Property Code

The Texas Property Code contains the following procedures for nonjudicial foreclosure. You can check what your area procedures are by contacting a real estate attorney or your local title insurance company.

1. The trustee must notify the debtor of the foreclosure sale at least 21 days before the date of the sale. This notice is to be sent by certified mail to the debtor's last known address.
2. Notice must be posted at the courthouse door of the county in which the property is located and filed in the county clerk's office where the sale is to be held.
3. The sale must be a public auction held between 10:00 A.M. and 4:00 P.M. on the first Tuesday of the month.
4. The sale must take place in the county where the property is located.
5. The holder of the debt on residential property must give the debtor at least 20 days to cure the default before the entire debt can be accelerated and declared due and the notice of sale given.

## At the Foreclosure Sale

At the foreclosure sale, the trustee has an obligation to act impartially and can take no action that would discourage bidders. This is to be a public auction open to all persons, including the lender and the trustee.

There is no requirement in Texas that the auction generate fair market value; therefore, the property will go to the highest cash bidder. The purchaser of the foreclosed property takes the title without any covenants through an instrument called a trustee's deed.

The proceeds from the sale will be used to pay the trustee and any expenses of the trustee's sale. Then the lender who is foreclosing will be paid. If there is any money left, those creditors who had filed liens against the property will be paid. Finally, any surplus monies must be returned to the borrower/debtor.

In Texas, as in every other state in the United States, if a senior lien holder forecloses, all junior lien holders' interests terminate. If a junior lien forecloses, the holder gets the title to the property subject to the senior lien holder's interest in the property. Our international readers can check local customary actions for terminating liens. Now let's talk about judicial foreclosure and sale.

## Judicial Foreclosure and Sale

Judicial foreclosure and sale is a legal procedure that involves the use of the courts and the consequent sale of the collateral. Foreclosure by court order is an alternative method that may be used in Texas, and other places, although it is not favored by commercial lenders. It is the only remedy if a deed of trust does not contain a power of sale provision.

### How a Judicial Foreclosure and Sale Works

The delinquent mortgagors are notified of the default and the reasons for it.

They are also informed that an immediate solution is required and that all their efforts must be expended to solve the problem as quickly as possible.

However, if all attempts fail, a complaint is filed by the lender in the court for the county in which the property is located and a summons is issued to the borrowers. This initiates the foreclosure process.

Simultaneous with this activity, a title search is made to determine the identities of all the parties having an interest in the collateral property, and a *lis pendens* (literally, a legal action pending) is filed with the court, giving notice to the world of the pending foreclosure action.

Notice is sent to all parties having an interest in the property requesting that they appear in court in order to defend their interests, or else they will be foreclosed (shut out, excluded, barred, or deprived) from any future rights by judgment of the court. It is vitally important for the complainant lender to notify all junior lien holders of the foreclosure action so they will not be enjoined from participation in the property auction. If junior lien holders are not given proper notice, they acquire the right to file suit on their own at some future time.

### *Jurisdiction*

Once the requisite number of days required by the presiding jurisdiction for public notice to be given to inform any and all persons having an unrecorded interest in the subject property that a foreclosure suit is imminent and a court date is set, the complaint is eventually aired before a presiding judge. In most instances, the defendant borrower does not appear in court unless special circumstances are presented in defense of the default.

Those creditors who do appear to present their claims are recognized and noted, and a sale of the property at a public auction by a court-appointed referee or the sheriff is ordered by means of a judgment decree. The proceeds from the sale will be used to satisfy the parties named in the judgment. The borrower's right to redeem the property continues for a reasonable time after the sale.

In a judicial foreclosure a junior lien holder's interest in the property is not automatically eliminated. If the junior lien holder did not join in the foreclosure suit, the property is sold subject to the junior lien. If, however, the junior lien holder was a party to the foreclosure suit, this interest ends at the sale in the same way as the senior lien holder's interest does. Now we are going to look at insured mortgage foreclosures.

## Insured Conventional Mortgage Foreclosure

Under the terms of the insurance policies of most private mortgage guarantee companies (companies that sell private mortgage insurance), a default is declared after nonpayment for four months. Within 10 days of default, the lender is required to notify the private mortgage insurer, which will then decide whether or not to instruct the lender to foreclose.

When an insured conventional mortgage is foreclosed, the lender that is insured is the original bidder at the public auction of the collateral property. Under these circumstances, the lender with the successful bid files notice with the insurance company within 60 days after the legal proceedings have transpired.

### Loss Recovery

If the insurance company is confident of recovering any losses by purchasing the collateral property from the lender and then reselling it, it will reimburse the lender for the total amount of the lender's bid and receive title to the property.

If, however, the private mortgage insurance company does not foresee any possibility for recovery, it may elect to pay the lender the agreed upon amount of insurance, and the lender retains ownership of the property. The lender then sells the property to recover any balance still unpaid.

Private mortgage insurance will play a role in a lender's agreement to do a short-sale. If private mortgage insurance compensates the lender for part of the lender's loss, the lender may be willing to do a short-sale with you at a greatly reduced loan payoff.

Remember that, in any and all cases of judicial foreclosure and sale, any ownership rights acquired by the successful bidder at the foreclosure auction will still be subject to the statutory redemption rights of the defaulted mortgagor. A full fee, simple, absolute title cannot vest in the winning bidder until these redemption rights have expired.

A property title vests, or becomes valid, when you receive full ownership rights in a property. Another way to say this is that once there is a vesting of title, your interest in the property cannot be voided.

## FHA Insured Mortgage Foreclosure

In the United States, foreclosures on Federal Housing Administration (FHA) insured mortgages originate with the filing of form 2068 Notice of Default by the lender. This form must be given to the local FHA administrative office within 60 days of default. The notice describes the reasons for the mortgagor's delinquency, such as death, illness, marital difficulties, income loss, excessive financial obligations, employment transfers, or military service.

In many cases involving delinquent FHA insured mortgages, loan counselors from the local FHA office will attempt to broker an agreement between the lender and the borrower that makes adjustments to the loan conditions in order to prevent foreclosure. The most common technique used in circumstances in which default is beyond the borrower's control, but deemed curable, is known as forbearance of foreclosure.

Forbearance of foreclosure occurs when a lender does not file a foreclosure action even though the lender has the legal right to do so. The lender and borrower sign an agreement that stipulates how back payments will be handled. This allows the borrower to remain in the property.

### *Default Not Cured*

If the problems causing the default are solved within a one-year period, the lender informs the local FHA office of that fact. If not, a default status report is filed and the lender must initiate foreclosure proceedings. If the bids at the foreclosure auction are less than the unpaid mortgage balance, the lender is expected to bid the debt, take title to the property, and present it to the FHA along with a claim for insurance, which may be paid in cash or in government securities. In some case, with prior FHA approval, the lender may assign the defaulted mortgage directly to the FHA before the final foreclosure action in exchange for insurance benefits.

In any case, if the property can be sold easily at a price that would repay the loan in full, the lender simply would sell the property after winning the bid at the foreclosure auction and would not apply for FHA compensation. However, if the property cannot be sold at a price that would repay the loan in full, then the lender will involve FHA.

FHA, like most lenders, would prefer not to be in the property owning business. If FHA ends up as the owner of the property, the property may be sold "as is." FHA may repair or refurbish the property if it feels the property can be resold at a higher price and minimize the losses to FHA. FHA will consider participating in a short-sale. FHA will participate in a short-sale if it saves FHA money.

# VA Guaranteed Mortgage Foreclosure

Unlike the FHA insured mortgage, whereby a lender's entire risk is recovered from the insurance benefits, a Department of Veterans Affairs or VA loan is similar to a privately insured loan in that a lender receives only the top portion of the outstanding loan balance up to a statutory limit.

Let's say the veteran borrowed $100,000 from a VA-approved lender. The VA will guarantee the top $25,000. The lender will be responsible for the remaining $75,000. If the loss exceeds the VA guaranteed $25,000, the lender will be responsible for any excess above the $25,000.

### Lender Responsibility

| | |
|---|---|
| Amount borrowed | $100,000 |
| VA guaranteed | −25,000 |
| Lender responsibility | $ 75,000 |

In the event a delinquency of more than three months of payments on a VA loan, the lender must file proper notification with the local VA office, which may then elect to bring the loan current if it wishes. If this occurs, the VA can approach the defaulting veteran for repayment of the funds advanced.

## Like the FHA

Much like the FHA, VA lenders are required to make every effort to help the borrower through forbearance, payment adjustments, a deed in lieu of foreclosure (more about this shortly) or other acceptable solution. An actual foreclosure is only considered as a last resort.

In the event of a foreclosure, the lender usually will be the original bidder at the auction and will submit a claim for losses to the local VA office. The Department of Veterans Affairs has the option to pay the unpaid balance, interest, and any court costs, and then take title to the property.

The VA can require that the lender keep the property. It may do this if the property has badly deteriorated. This reinforces the importance that the lender supervise the condition of the property. The VA would pay the lender the difference between the determined value of the property on the date of the foreclosure sale and the remaining mortgage balance.

## Second Mortgage Foreclosure

Defaults of second mortgages and other junior mortgages are handled exactly in the same manner as conventional first mortgages. Here, however, the relationship is usually, but not always, between two individuals rather than between an institutional lender and an individual borrower.

A second mortgagee will usually seek the counsel of an attorney to manage the foreclosure process against a second mortgagor. The delinquent borrower will be requested to cure the problem within a certain time period. If a cure cannot be accomplished, notice is given to all persons having an interest in the property, and the attorney then files for judicial foreclosure.

The second mortgagee generally is the original bidder at the public sale and secures ownership of the collateral property subject to the lien of the existing first mortgage. It can then continue to maintain the integrity of this first mortgage by making any payments required, while seeking to sell the collateral to eliminate, or at least offset, any losses.

## Deficiency Judgments

If the proceeds from a foreclosure sale are not sufficient to recover the outstanding loan balance plus the costs incurred as a consequence of default and interest to date, a lender may, in most places, sue on the mortgage for the deficiency.

If the foreclosure is by court order, the judge normally awards the lender a judgment against the debtor in the amount of the deficiency. If a power of sale foreclosure took place, the lender must then file suit against the debtor to collect any deficiency.

For example, in Texas, a lender would consider several things before pursuing legal action for a deficiency balance because the amount of the deficiency and the ability of the debtor to pay after the suit would be important factors.

The homestead laws in Texas, as in many other places, would protect most of the debtor's basic possessions from this type of judgment. In most cases, a defaulted borrower does not have any nonexempt assets to make up this deficiency. Otherwise, those assets would have been put to use in order to prevent the default in the first place.

### Current Trend

The current trend is to rely less on collecting deficiencies and more on limiting a borrower's personal liability on a real estate loan to the equity in the collateral property. Especially on purchase money loans, lenders may be limited to recovering only the collateral property and nothing more.

Most borrowers initially borrow money to purchase real estate. These borrowers get into financial trouble in the initial two or three years. They typically have little or no equity built up in the property. All the lender can do is foreclose on the property.

If the sale of the property does not fully compensate the lender for what it is owed, that is too bad for the lender. The lender cannot go after the borrower personally for any deficiencies. (The one exception to this is that the VA can and will go after the defaulting veteran.) It may be in the lender's best interest to dispose of the property via a short-sale deal with us investors.

## Lender Adjustments

A lender will usually attempt to adjust the conditions of a loan in order to help a troubled borrower over short-term difficulties. Delinquent mortgage payments are the most common cause for a default. The nonpayment of property taxes or hazard insurance premiums, lack of adequate maintenance, and allowing priority liens to take effect are also cause for default.

To offset the possibility of a foreclosure on delinquent mortgages, many lenders will exercise forbearance and waive the principal portion of a loan payment for a while or even extend a moratorium on the full monthly payment until a borrower can better arrange his finances.

Other adjustments in terms of a delinquent mortgage that might aid the defaulting borrower include an extension of time or a recasting of the loan to reflect the borrower's current ability to pay under circumstances of financial distress.

### Take a Deed in Lieu of Foreclosure

A lender may encourage a hopelessly defaulted borrower to voluntarily give a deed to the property to the lender. This is called a deed in lieu of foreclosure. By executing either a quit claim deed or a grant deed, a borrower can eliminate the stigma of a foreclosure, maintain a respectable credit rating, and avoid the possibility of a deficiency judgment.

However, the lender must take care to be protected against any future claims of fraud or duress by the borrower. In addition, the lender must be aware of the possibility of the existence of other liens like IRS (revenue tax) liens filed against the property.

### Sell the Mortgage

Sometimes all efforts at adjusting the terms of a mortgage to solve a borrower's problems fail. A lender may then attempt to sell the loan rather than foreclose. This creates another opportunity for you as a real estate investor.

### Do a Short-Sale

Real estate lenders are fully aware of the difficulties with and the costs and time involved in a full foreclosure process. A good estimate of the cost for a lender to start and complete a foreclosure sale is $20,000. This makes a lender open to an investor willing to do a short-sale. The short-sale allows the lender to avoid the costly and time-consuming process of foreclosure.

This chapter provides an overview of the foreclosure process. Most real estate financing arrangements do not result in problems leading to foreclosure.

Historically rising property values coupled with the systematic repayment of loans created measurable equity positions for borrowers. A troubled borrower could, in most problem situations, arrange to dispose of his or her property and thus maintain financial equilibrium.

This is what gives you, as a real estate investor, an opportunity to help someone in financial distress and still make a profit. When misfortune cannot be avoided and foreclosure looms on the horizon, this provides the motivation to the borrower with equity to be open to your help.

Recently, because of overly aggressive lending practices including interest-only or negatively amortized loans, which may cause properties to go underwater, and the crashing of most real estate markets, there are borrowers without a measurable equity position in their properties who are getting into a financial bind. This is what is creating the unprecedented short-sale investment opportunity.

### *Government Intervention*

As we mentioned in Chapter 1, in the United States the federal government is intervening in the real estate market to help four to five million homeowners keep their homes. However, there are at least another five to seven million homeowners who are underwater and who will not be able to keep their homes. This is our target real estate investment market for the next 48 months.

In Chapter 4 we explain the new foreclosure strategy centered on short-sales. Equipped with the knowledge and information in this book you will be positioned to take complete advantage of this historic short-sale opportunity. A short-sale is a lender agreeing to a sale of a property for less than the loan amount the lender is owed on the property. A short-sale allows you to be able to buy property at a wholesale price.

# CHAPTER 4

# The New Foreclosure Tactics

The new foreclosure tactics are to concentrate your investment efforts on short-sales. A short-sale is actually a preforeclosure sale. Any property that has a real estate loan attached to it is a short-sale waiting to happen. When a property owner has a mortgage greater than the value of the property, he is said to be underwater and thus a prime candidate for a short-sale.

A short-sale occurs when a lender agrees to sell a property for less than the remaining loan amount. The lender who agrees to do a short-sale appears to be taking a bath. Your job is to convince the lender that it is in the lender's best interest to agree to do a short-sale with you.

The old tactics are to buy foreclosure property on the courthouse steps. At the foreclosure sale the lender's opening credit bid is always for more than the loan amount. Stop buying properties at these white elephant sales. You may get stuck feeding them. Or worse, they may start feeding on you!

It is worth reiterating here that the United States federal government plans to intervene in the real estate market to help four to five million homeowners keep their homes. This will leave at least another five to seven million homeowners who are underwater and who will not be able to keep their homes. This is our target real estate investment market for the next 48 months.

# Short-Sales

Once you understand short-sales from the lender's point of view you are in a position to package your short-sale offer. We recommend using a checklist to make sure you include everything necessary to have your short-sale offer accepted by the lender.

We first present our short-sale offer checklist in a narrative fashion. We will expand on some of the points of the checklist so that you have a detailed understanding. You may find that you want to add or subtract items to your short-sale checklist depending upon any unique circumstances concerning the property you are seeking to acquire by short-sale.

The point of the short-sale checklist is to facilitate your assembling the paperwork and documents necessary to present the best possible short-sale submission package to the lender. The more complete your submission package the easier it will be for the lender to accept your short-sale offer. We want you to keep the lender from doing any deal except yours.

# The Short-Sale Checklist

Our short-sale checklist consists of 18 items. Notice that there are 14 items before we get to the actual short-sale real estate purchase contract. This includes an owner financial statement, an owner financial history, owner payroll stubs, and copies of the previous two years of owner tax returns. Also, get copies of the last six months of the owner's bank statements, a copy of his unemployment award letter, and copies of unpaid medical bills.

Then assemble a market analysis of market comparable properties (comps) showing the lowest sales in the area that were similar to the property we are interested in buying, fill out a HUD 1 closing statement (or whatever it may be called in your country), put together two repair cost estimates, and take pictures of the property. These pictures should show the property in its worst possible light.

### Short-Sale Checklist

1. Your short-sale proposal letter.
2. Signed borrower authorization to release information.

3.  Borrower's signed short-sale payoff application.
4.  Owner hardship letter.
5.  Owner financial statement.
6.  Owner financial history.
7.  Owner payroll stubs.
8.  Two years of owner tax returns.
9.  Six months of owner bank statements.
10. Owner credit reports.
11. Unemployment benefits or status.
12. Medical bills.
13. Divorce decree.
14. Signed owner/borrower short-sale purchase contracts.
15. Market comparables.
16. HUD 1 closing statement (or appropriate form for your country).
17. Repair cost estimates.
18. As-is pictures.

## Short-Sale Examples

We will use an actual short-sale deal for an example to make the short-sale checklist come alive for you. We found an owner who was four months behind on his $3,200 monthly mortgage payment for a total of $12,800.

The amount outstanding on the loan was $600,000. The lender was about to foreclose. The lender would like to receive the $600,000 loan balance plus $12,800 for the four back payments.

### Lender Desired Payoff

| | |
|---|---|
| Loan balance | $600,000 |
| Back payments | +12,800 |
| Lender desired payoff | $612,800 |

The property was worth $510,000. The owner was underwater $102,800.

### Owner Underwater

| | |
|---|---|
| Property value | $510,000 |
| Lender desired payoff | −612,800 |
| Owner underwater | −$102,800 |

Assuming the owner could sell the property for $510,000 the closing costs would be in the $35,000 to $40,000 range (real estate commissions, escrow fees, attorneys' fees, and title insurance). The owner did not have the $12,800 to make up the back payments let alone the $40,000 needed to sell the property.

As real estate investors, it appeared that there was no way for us to make money in this situation either. Our competition definitely thought there was no way to make money on this deal. Actually, we had no competition because 90 to 95 percent of our competition had already walked away.

### The Short-Sale Deal

We made a deal with the owner to buy his property for $439,000. We explained to the owner that we would have to have the lender agree to do a short-sale. This would be the only way we could buy the owner's property. If the lender would not agree to do a short-sale there would be no deal.

There were several benefits to the owner if he agreed to accept our short-sale offer. The owner would not have to make up the $12,800 in back payments. He would also not have to put the additional $40,000 into selling the property. This would save the owner $52,800 in out-of-pocket expenses.

### Owner Savings

| | |
|---|---|
| Back payments | $12,800 |
| Additional owner money | +40,000 |
| Owner savings | $52,800 |

The owner would be out from under the impending lender foreclosure. He would not have to pay off the remaining loan balance. There would be no foreclosure sale against the owner's credit rating.

We had the owner sign our real estate purchase contract. We had the owner sign an authorization to release information from the lender. We helped him write a hardship letter. Then, using the short-sale checklist, we went about assembling the remaining information and documentation for our short-sale submission package.

## Your Short-Sale Proposal Letter

We recommend you write a short-sale proposal letter to accompany your short-sale offer. This letter is a one-page synopsis of your short-sale purchase contract. This proposal letter should be placed at the top of the submissions package and should be the first thing the lender sees. Here is a sample short-sale proposal letter.

---

Short-Sale Proposal for
711 Lucky Street
Oceanside, USA

July 22, 2009

To: The Loss Mitigation Department of ABC Lending Company
Attention: Samantha Sanchez, Loss Mitigation Specialist
From: Bill and Chantal Carey 817.555.2345
Regarding: 711 Lucky Street, Oceanside, USA

Dear Ms. Sanchez,

We have a signed real estate purchase contract with your borrower Liam O'Rourke, the owner of 711 Lucky Street, Oceanside, USA. Mr. O'Rourke has agreed to sell us his property for a purchase price of $439,000.

Your current loan balance for loan 78934564321 is $600,000. Mr. O'Rourke is four payments behind in the amount of $12,800. He has lost his job as a systems analyst and is receiving unemployment compensation.

We have provided comparable sales of properties in the area. We feel that after you do an analysis of the numbers, you will realize that it is in your best interest to accept our all-cash offer. We look forward to doing business with you.

Sincerely,

Bill and Chantal Carey

---

## Signed Borrower Authorization to Release Information

You must have a signed borrower authorization to release information before the borrower/owner's lender can legally talk to you. This authorization to release information can be very simple. Here is the authorization to release information filled out for this transaction.

---

### AUTHORIZATION TO RELEASE INFORMATION

I/We _____ Liam O'Rourke _____ , the
borrower(s) of record for loan number <u>78934564321</u> give you
<u>ABC Lending Company</u> , our lender of record, written authoriza-
tion to release information regarding our loan to <u>Chantal or Bill
Carey</u> .

Signed and dated this <u>22</u><sup>nd</sup> day of <u>July</u> , <u>2009</u> .

<u>Liam O'Rourke</u>        _____
  Borrower         Borrower

---

## Borrower's Signed Short-Sale Payoff Application

The short-sale payoff application is provided by the lender. You may have
obtained this in advance of your putting together your short-sale submission package. If that is the case, you will have the borrower/owner
fill out and sign the short-sale payoff application and submit it as part of
your package.

Some lenders will provide this to the borrower/owner only after
receiving the submission package. If this is the case, we recommend you
help the borrower/owner fill it out. Make sure he signs it. Then take the
application and scan and e-mail, fax, or mail it to the lender.

Do not wait for the borrower/owner to do anything. You must be
proactive or your short-sale deal will die for lack of timely follow-
through. Remember the borrower/owner is already in trouble and may
not be operating with his normally balanced emotional status.

## Owner Hardship Letter

The hardship letter serves two purposes. The first purpose is to present
you as the lender's solution to a potential full-blown foreclosure problem. The problem for the lender is winding up owning the property

after no one bids at the foreclosure sale. Your short-sale offer is the solution to the lender's problem.

The second purpose the hardship letter serves is it salvages the owner/borrower's financial situation to the extent possible given its distressed condition. By agreeing to a short-sale the owner/borrower avoids the damage of an actual foreclosure sale on his credit reports.

We are going to give you an example of an owner/borrower hardship letter. An effective hardship letter sticks to the facts and is straightforward and relatively simple. Typically, there are stringent hardship tests for owner/borrowers to satisfy in order for a lender to authorize a short-sale.

---

### HARDSHIP LETTER

July 22, 2009

To Whom It May Concern,

This is a hardship letter. I lost my job as a systems analyst. I have been unemployed for six months. I have been receiving unemployment benefits. However, my unemployment check replaces about one quarter of my previous income. I have exhausted my savings. My credit cards are maxed out. I am seriously contemplating filing for bankruptcy protection.

I can no longer afford to make the $3,200 monthly mortgage payment on my home. I am currently four months behind. I see no way to make up the $12,800 in back payments. The value of my home is almost $100,000 less than my mortgage balance.

I am interested in selling my property to Chantal and Bill Carey. I want to avoid a foreclosure sale that will further damage my credit. I request you work with Mr. and Mrs. Carey to negotiate a short-sale transaction.

This would be in my best interest financially. I am willing to cooperate with you as my lender to provide whatever documentation that you require in order to make this short-sale happen.

Sincerely,

Liam O'Rourke
Owner/Borrower

These include illness, death, divorce, job transfer, military service, disability, unemployment, incarceration, and insolvency. According to the Internal Revenue Service, "You are insolvent when, and to the extent, your liabilities exceed the fair market value of your assets."

Another word for insolvency is bankruptcy. In the United States, under the Homeowner's Stability Initiative, federal bankruptcy judges may have the authority to cram down the mortgage balance or modify the mortgage terms for a homeowner in bankruptcy. The hardship letter is a powerful way to get the lender's attention and stimulate the lender's interest in a short-sale deal.

## Owner Financial Statement

An owner financial statement can be very simply constructed. An owner financial statement lists all the owner's assets including real estate, stocks, bonds, mutual funds, collectibles, and bank accounts. Then it lists all the owner's liabilities such as the current real estate loan that is in arrears, personal loans, credit card debt, lawsuits, judgments, and IRS liens.

In our experience we have found that the owner's liabilities usually exceed his assets. Sometimes this can be by a substantial amount. Mr. O'Rourke's financial statement certainly fell into this category.

### Owner Financial Statement

| Assets | | Liabilities |
|---|---|---|
| $510,000 | Real Estate Owned | |
| | Real Estate Loan | $600,000 |
| | Back Monthly Payments | 13,000 |
| | Credit Card Debt | 19,700 |
| 15,000 | Car | |
| | Car Loan | 17,000 |
| | Medical Bills | 4,300 |
| $525,000 | | $654,000 |

When your liabilities exceed your assets you are said to have a negative net worth. Mr. O'Rourke net worth was a negative $129,000.

**Net Worth**

| | |
|---|---|
| Assets | $525,000 |
| Liabilities | −654,000 |
| Net worth | −$129,000 |

Some lenders want you to include all the monthly expenses in addition to the assets and liabilities. This would include house payments, car payments, utility bills, credit card bills, medical bills, insurance costs, tuition expenses, child support, food, and clothing—anything that the borrower is obligated to pay monthly.

## Owner Financial History

Mr. O'Rourke's financial history was not good. He had been experiencing a series of financial setbacks for the past 18 months. He had lost his job. His unemployment benefits had run out. He was borrowing from one credit card to make the monthly payment on another credit card. He was four months behind on his mortgage payments. He was contemplating bankruptcy.

If you encounter an owner who files for bankruptcy protection after he has agreed to sell you his property, you may have to alter your short-sale plans. The bankruptcy court has the final say as to whether your short-sale will go through.

The bankruptcy judge has the power to make the lender accept a payment plan from the borrower/owner if he decides he wants to keep the property. Or the judge may request the lender to cram down the loan balance or change the terms of the loan including the monthly payment, loan term, and interest rate.

## Owner Payroll Stubs

For this deal there were no pay stubs to provide. The borrower/owner was unemployed. If Mr. O'Rourke were employed, providing the pay stubs as part of the submission package would allow the lender to see if the monthly take home pay would cover the loan payments plus all the other monthly expenses.

## Two Years of Owner Tax Returns

The lender will request the last one to two years of the borrower/owner's federal income tax returns. The lender is trying to get a complete picture of the borrower/owner's financial situation. Is the income going up? Is the income going down? Will Mr. O'Rourke be able to make loan payments if the lender agrees to a repayment program? Does Mr. O'Rourke want to continue making payments? Mr. O'Rourke made it very clear to us that he was not interested in continuing to make any more loan payments. He wanted out, period.

## Six Months of Owner Bank Statements

The six months of bank statements is again so the lender can determine if the borrower/owner is capable of making loan payments. Mr. O'Rourke's bank statements provided more evidence that the lender should do the short-sale deal with us. In other words, the bank statements showed he had no money.

## Owner Credit Reports

Owner credit reports will be ordered by the lender. Mr. O'Rourke's credit reports reflected his financial condition. All the credit cards were at their credit limit. Some of the accounts were 30, 60, and 90 days past due.

Rather than this being a negative for the deal, this was a positive for the deal. The lender realized that Mr. O'Rourke was not going to be in a position to make the mortgage payments anytime soon. This contributed to the lender agreeing to a short-sale.

## Unemployment Benefits or Status

A borrower/owner receiving unemployment benefits or being unemployed are positive indicators for your short-sale going through. Lenders are under political pressure to extend every effort to borrowers for some type of loan workout.

However, when it becomes obvious that the borrower has no financial wherewithal, the lender is off the proverbial hook. Mr. O'Rourke's unemployment status was a major contributing factor in the lender agreeing to do a short-sale.

## Medical Hardship

Unfortunately, a medical need or condition with the attendant medical bills can be the reason for a borrower/owner getting into financial difficulty. If you encounter a property owner in this situation, a short-sale may be the best solution for him to get out from under a now too-large mortgage payment.

Medical hardships are easy for a lender to understand. Lenders will agree to a short-sale in just about every medical hardship situation. In fact, we have never heard of a lender not agreeing to a short-sale if the borrower/owner was experiencing a medical hardship and requested the lender to participate with an investor in a short-sale offer.

## Divorce Decree

The number one reason people get into financial difficulty is a divorce situation. Instead of one monthly house payment, there now may be two monthly house payments. The likelihood of the lender approving a short-sale goes up dramatically when the borrowers are in a divorce situation.

## Signed Owner/Borrower Short-Sale Purchase Contract

This one is obvious. You have to have the borrower/owner's signature on a short-sale purchase contract before you can ask the lender to agree to a short-sale. The borrower/owner is still the owner of the property. The lender cannot sell you the property. The lender doesn't own the property.

## Market Comparables

The lender will order one or two Broker Price Opinions after it receives your short-sale submission package. We have found that it will only help your cause if you provide your own market comparables. Of course, you will provide only the lowest comparables for the area of the property for which you are making your short-sale offer.

We want to make note here of an interesting phenomenon. We are finding that most of the short-sales we are doing are with properties that are less than five years old. Unlike the stereotypical run-down or dilapidated foreclosure properties, the short-sale properties we are buying are in good to excellent shape. This means that it is relatively simple to determine the value of the property.

## HUD 1 Closing Statement (or Appropriate Form for Your Country)

The Department of Housing and Urban Development (HUD) has created a standardized closing statement that is used throughout the United States. This is a net sheet that lists all the credits and debits for a buyer or seller involved in a real estate transaction.

By including a net sheet in your submission package you give the lender the bottom-line dollars at the closing of the transaction. This is the figure the person in the loss mitigation department needs to know before she can approve your short-sale offer.

You may have asked the lender to pay for things such as title insurance, half the escrow fee, attorney fees, termite inspections, and repairs. All these will reduce the net cash the lender will receive.

## Repair Cost Estimates

As we have noted, we are buying short-sale properties that are relatively new. Therefore, we have found that we have minor repairs to make to the property in most cases.

However, if you are faced with a major repair, we recommend you ask the lender to pay for it in your short-sale offer. After all, the lender is going to have to pay for repairs if it forecloses and winds up taking the property back as a real estate owned property.

## As-Is Pictures

The expression, "a picture is worth a thousand words," is even truer with your short-sale package. If you are buying a property that is dilapidated or in need of repairs, by all means take pictures of the unsightly areas.

You are not trying to downgrade or devalue the property. You are trying to make the lender aware of the true condition of the property. Obviously, any money you have to spend to return the property to a good and sellable or rentable condition has to be factored into your short-sale offer.

In the next chapter we are going to take you inside the loss mitigation departments of real estate lenders. By understanding short-sales from the lender's point of view, you will be able to communicate more effectively with the lender's short-sale decision maker. It is this decision maker who will make or break your short-sale deal. We will let you know the outcome of our short-sale offer example in Chapter 7: Lender Acceptance and Closing.

# CHAPTER 5

# Inside the Loss
# Mitigation Department

In this chapter we are going to take you inside the loss mitigation departments of real estate lenders. By understanding short-sales from the lender's point of view, you will be able to communicate more effectively with the lender's short-sale decision maker.

## 12 Short-Sale Lender Factors

We are going to present the 12 factors that a lender will consider before accepting a short-sale offer. The better understanding you have of these 12 factors, the more effective you will be in putting together your short-sale package. The more effective your short-sale package, the more likely the lender will agree to accept your short-sale offer.

The 12 short-sale factors that a lender will consider include the number of lender nonperforming loans, the lender financial condition, the third party investor's financial condition, the third-party investor's loss mitigation department, the servicing lenders, the borrower's finances, mortgage insurance, and the as-is value of the property. And finally, it will look at the costs to repair the property for resale, the repaired value, the cost of securing and maintaining the property, and the cost of holding and selling the property.

### 12 Short-Sale Lender Factors

1. Number of lender nonperforming loans.
2. Lender financial condition.
3. Third-party investor's financial condition.
4. Third-party investor's loss mitigation department.
5. Servicing lenders.
6. Borrower's finances.
7. Mortgage insurance.
8. As-is value of property.
9. Costs to repair property for resale.
10. Repaired value.
11. Cost of securing and maintaining property.
12. Cost of holding and selling property.

## Number of Lender Nonperforming Loans

A performing loan is a loan a lender has on its financial statement as an asset. The loan is considered a performing loan when the lender is receiving payments as scheduled.

A nonperforming loan is a loan that a lender has on its financial statement as a liability. The loan is considered a nonperforming loan when the lender is receiving no payments as scheduled.

Every lender must maintain an acceptable financial statement to remain in business. If a lender is carrying too high a percentage of nonperforming loans on its financial statement the lender gets in trouble with the federal lending regulators.

As the real estate market has crashed, lenders have experienced a huge increase in the number of nonperforming loans. This will contribute to greater opportunities for short-sale deals to be made with lenders that are accumulating a logjam of these loans. A lender's acceptance of your short-sale offer wipes a nonperforming loan in the lender's loan portfolio off its financial statement.

## Lender Financial Condition

Federal lending regulators give real estate lenders a grace period to have nonperforming loans become performing loans again before the nonperforming loans become a lender financial statement liability. This grace period is typically 180 days (six months).

Nonperforming loans are still counted as assets for the lender during the grace period. After the grace period ends, the nonperforming loans are shifted from the asset side of the lender's financial statement to the liability side of the lender's financial statement. This is a bad thing for the lender.

If a lender can do a short-sale with a nonperforming loan before the grace period ends, the nonperforming loan never moves over to the liability side of the financial statement. We recommend you bring this information to the attention of the person you are dealing with in the lender's loss mitigation department. This may help that individual make the case to his superiors to get your short-sale deal accepted. After all, his job is to mitigate lender losses (liabilities). You are helping him do his job when you give him an opportunity to accept your short-sale offer!

## *Example*

Let's say we have a bank that has $310 million in real estate mortgages. These mortgages are regarded as assets while they are performing. As we have said, they are also regarded as assets for 180 days if they are nonperforming.

The bank has $170 million in deposits, which, while they are necessary for the bank to be able to make loans, are regarded as liabilities on the financial statement. This makes sense when you realize that the deposits are assets of the depositors and do not belong to the bank. The bank also is listing $30 million in bad debts, which is obviously a liability.

### Bank Financial Statement
### As of 7/22/09

| Assets | | Liabilities |
|---|---|---|
| $310 Million | Real Estate Mortgages | |
| | Deposits | $170 Million |
| | Bad Debts | 30 Million |
| | Net Worth | 110 Million |
| $310 Million | | $310 Million |

Another name for a financial statement is a balance sheet. The assets are equal to the liabilities plus the net worth. Put another way:

**Assets minus liabilities equals net worth.**

Looking at this financial statement, you can see there are $310 million in assets minus $200 million in liabilities, which equals $110 million net worth.

### Net Worth

| | |
|---|---|
| Assets | $310 million |
| Liabilities | −200 million |
| Net worth | $110 million |

What happens if $125 million of real estate mortgages, which have been nonperforming, go past 180 days on September 9, 2009? They would then be considered bad debts and would have to be moved from the asset side to the liability side. Now the bad debts amount goes up from $30 million to $155 million.

### Bad Debts as of 9/9/09

| | |
|---|---|
| Bad debts as of 7/22/09 | $ 30 million |
| Additional bad debts | +125 million |
| Bad debts as of 9/9/09 | $155 million |

The assets drop from $310 million to $185 million.

### Assets as of 9/9/09

| | |
|---|---|
| Assets as of 7/22/09 | $310 million |
| Nonperforming assets/bad debts | −125 million |
| Assets as of 9/9/09 | $185 million |

The net worth drops from $110 million to a negative $140 million.

### Net Worth as of 9/9/09

| | |
|---|---|
| Assets as of 9/9/09 | $185 million |
| Liabilities as of 9/9/09 | −325 million |
| Net worth as of 9/9/09 | −$140 million |

This becomes a double whammy to the bank's financial statement.

**Bank Financial Statement**
**As of 9/9/09**

| Assets | | Liabilities |
|---|---|---|
| $185 Million | Real Estate Mortgages | |
| | Deposits | $170 Million |
| | Bad Debts | 155 Million |
| | Net Worth | −140 Million |
| $185 Million | | $185 Million |

At first glance everything still looks good. The bank has $185 million in assets. It is not until you look more closely that you realize this bank is now underwater with liabilities exceeding assets in the amount of $140 million!

**Net Worth**

| | |
|---|---|
| Assets | $185 million |
| Liabilities | −325 million |
| Net worth | (−$140 million) |

## Third-Party Investor's Financial Condition

You will find that four out of five short-sale opportunities involve a third-party investor who has purchased the loan from the original lender. These third-party investors operate in the secondary mortgage market. As we have said, the secondary mortgage market was created in the United States in the 1930s in response to the failure of banks and thrifts during the depression.

Now, the banks could turn around and sell the mortgage paper to Fannie Mae for cash. Fannie Mae packages the millions of dollars of mortgage paper and creates a pool of securities that are backed by the mortgages. Fannie Mae then sells these mortgage-backed securities to large institutional investors to get its cash back. And the cycle repeats.

### The Primary and Secondary Mortgage Market

Money →                                              ←  Money
        Primary                                    Secondary
Borrowers ~~~~~~ Lenders ~~~~~~ Fannie Mae ~~~~~~ Investors
        Market                                        Market
Paper →                                              ←  Paper

Entities like Fannie Mae and Freddie Mac are third-party investors. Because both Fannie Mae and Freddie Mac have increased exposure to foreclosures and nonperforming real estate loans they were taken over by the United States government in 2008. As you make short-sale offers in the United States you will wind up dealing with these third-party investors.

## Third-Party Investor's Loss Mitigation Department

First there was the borrower and the lender. When the original lender sells his mortgage paper on the secondary mortgage market the original lender becomes the servicing lender for the third party-investor (Fannie Mae or Freddie Mac). If there is to be a short-sale the third-party investor's loss mitigation department will be involved.

Fannie Mae and Freddie Mac are willing to pursue a short-sale at any time prior to the actual foreclosure sale. They will do this if their acquisition of the property is the most likely situation at the foreclosure sale. Fannie Mae will proceed with the short-sale if the proceeds of the short-sale, along with the mortgage insurance settlement (if any), will make it whole or result in a loss less than the one that would be incurred if the property were acquired at the foreclosure sale.

Freddie Mac will approve a short-sale offer that is 90 to 92 percent of the broker's price opinion (BPO). Once Freddie Mac has the submission package, it will take two to three weeks to get a BPO ordered and processed.

## Freddie Mac Short-Sale

Let's look at a Freddie Mac short-sale. We found a property that had been on the market for six months. The owners had moved out of town. We contacted the owners and discovered the property was about to go to a foreclosure sale. The owners had written a hardship letter to their servicing lender and included the keys to the property!

We received the owner's permission to contact their servicing lender. The file had been dormant for three months. No one in the loss mitigation department knew what to do with the property once they realized the owners had sent the keys.

### Loss Mitigation Contact Person

We told the contact person in the loss mitigation department we wanted to make a short-sale offer. She told us that Freddie Mac was the third-party investor on the loan. We would have to work with Freddie Mac guidelines. She also told us there was mortgage insurance on the loan.

The owners initially had the property listed with a real estate broker for $249,000. The property was five years old. It had four bedrooms with three bathrooms. It contained 2,965 square feet of living area. At the list price the property was valued at $84 a square foot.

### Listed Price

| | |
|---|---|
| Square footage | 2,965 |
| Price per square foot | × $84 |
| Listed price | $249,000 |

Unfortunately the real estate market had cooled in the area. After the listing expired, the owners dropped the price 29 percent from $249,000 to $178,000 or $60 a square foot. They also dropped the real estate broker and decided to sell the property themselves. This is where we came in.

### Market Value

| | |
|---|---|
| Square footage | 2,965 |
| Price per square foot | × $60 |
| Market value | $178,000 |

### Fixer-Upper

When we got into the property we discovered it was a fixer-upper. Carpeting needed to be replaced. The kitchen countertops and floor were blue (not the good kind) and would have to go. The entire inside and outside of the property needed to be painted. The market comparable sales were in the $65 to $70 a square foot range for a value of $192,725.

### Comparable Value

| | |
|---|---|
| Square footage | 2,965 |
| Price per square foot | × $65 |
| Comparable value | $192,725 |

## Our Offer

We wrote our offer for $40 a square foot, which was $118,600.

### Our Offer

| | |
|---|---|
| Square footage | 2,965 |
| Price per square foot | × $40 |
| Our offer | $118,600 |

We had our offer signed by the owners and submitted our offer to the servicing lender. The servicing lender sent copies of the offer to Freddie Mac and the mortgage insurance company.

## Broker's Price Opinion

The BPO came back at $148,250 or $50 a square foot. Ninety-two percent of $148,250 is $136,400. This was the counteroffer we received from Freddie Mac.

### Freddie Mac Counter Offer

| | |
|---|---|
| Broker price opinion | $148,250 |
| Freddie Mac percentage | × 92% |
| Freddie Mac counteroffer | $136,400 |

## Counteroffer

We were $17,800 apart. We countered Freddie Mac's counteroffer at $124,900. Freddie Mac accepted the $124,900. We wound up paying $42 a square foot.

### Our Counteroffer

| | |
|---|---|
| Square footage | 2,965 |
| Price per square foot | × $42 |
| Our counteroffer | $124,900 |

## Fix-Up Costs

We replaced the carpet, painted the inside and outside of the house, and left the blue kitchen alone. We spent $5,100 in fix-up costs. We now had $130,000 invested in this property.

**Invested in Property**

| | |
|---|---|
| Counteroffer | $124,900 |
| Fix-up costs | + 5,100 |
| Invested in property | $130,000 |

## Property Auction

We then held an auction (see Chapter 11: No Doubt Getting Out) and sold the property for $178,000 or $60 a square foot. We made $48,000 on this Freddie Mac short-sale.

**Our Profit**

| | |
|---|---|
| Auction price | $178,000 |
| Money invested | − 130,000 |
| Our profit | $ 48,000 |

## Listing Broker

We usually prefer dealing directly with owners in our short-sale investing. However, you need to be prepared to deal with real estate brokers. They are part of the short-sale landscape. You may come upon a short-sale opportunity after the real estate broker is already on the scene.

Once the borrower/owner has worked with the servicing lender and Fannie Mae or Freddie Mac to determine that he or she is eligible for a short-sale, the borrower/owner may select a listing broker and execute a listing agreement. All parts of the listing agreement are between the broker and the borrower/owner and are not negotiated by the servicing lender, Fannie Mae, or Freddie Mac.

Fannie Mae recommends that the listing broker be prepared to distribute the submission package and real estate purchase contract to all involved institutions concurrently. These include the servicing lender, the mortgage insurance company (where applicable), and Fannie Mae. We agree with Fannie Mae's recommendation.

The submission of the information to all institutions at one time will help to expedite the acceptance and approval process. However, the listing agent's direct contact must always be with the borrower and the servicing lender. The listing broker should provide any assistance necessary to the borrower/owner in the preparation of the complete submission package.

You may want to develop a relationship with a real estate broker or professional consultant who specializes in short-sales with third-party investors. This can save you a lot of time and money. The broker or professional consultant can lead you to short-sale opportunities and can put together the short-sale submission package.

### For-Sale-By-Owner

If you are working with a property owner who is a for-sale-by-owner then there is no listing broker involved. Remember, the initial offer on the property must be made to the borrower, who is the owner of the property, and must negotiate as such.

Once you have an accepted contract you then contact the servicing lender and present your real estate purchase contract signed by the property owner, in copy form, to the servicing lender, Fannie Mae, or Freddie Mac, and the mortgage insurer (if applicable), concurrently.

## Servicing Lenders

Be prepared to deal with a servicing lender who is collecting the scheduled payments for a third-party investor like Fannie Mae or Freddie Mac. You will have to go through the servicing lender to deal with the third-party investor. The servicing lender is not the final decision maker for your short-sale deal.

However, all contact must be through the servicing lender. Fannie Mae's decision and any loss mitigation will be done through the servicing lender contact person only. If the short-sale submission is distributed in its complete form to all parties concurrently, you can expect a response within two to three weeks.

Be certain to allow for this amount of time in your real estate contracts.

When Fannie Mae has received a real estate purchase contract for a short-sale, it will provide in writing to the servicing lender its approval and authorization for a short payoff. It should be pointed out that Fannie Mae does not actively negotiate or sign any of the purchase contracts. Fannie Mae can only agree to the amount of the loss it will approve.

## Borrower's Finances

There are additional items that will be requested by the lender from the property owner besides the real estate purchase contract. Coordinating the distribution of these items will help expedite the decision making process.

### *Submission Package*

The submission package should include the borrower's letter of hardship, current financial statement, current pay stub, and the prior year's tax return. If the borrower is self-employed, he will need to include a copy of a year-to-date profit and loss statement, all schedules to the tax return, and a copy of any partnership or corporate tax returns, if applicable.

Fannie Mae will request copies of the current payoff statement, collection records, payment history, mortgage insurance information, and the origination documents from the servicing lender. This would also include the original mortgage application package and appraisal.

## Mortgage Insurance

After Fannie Mae or Freddie Mac receives the complete submission package, it will work with the servicing lender. They will also coordinate with the mortgage insurance company to determine any preclaim settlement agreement and negotiate the mitigation of their loss.

Once all the information has been received, Fannie Mae or Freddie Mac will coordinate with all parties through the servicing lender. Depending on their financial statement, there may be a requirement for the borrower to participate in the reduction of any potential loss to Fannie Mae or Freddie Mac by signing a promissory note.

## As-Is Value of Property

The as-is value of the property is determined using the existing condition of the property with no repairs or deferred maintenance being done. Two BPOs are ordered. These may be compared with the original appraisal to see the deterioration, if any, of the value of the property.

Broker price opinions are used in lieu of paying for a formal appraisal.

The lender relies on these BPOs as an indication of the comparative market value of the property in the current real estate market.

The servicing lender is responsible for ordering the two BPOs. They must be ordered from two separate sources that are not involved in the listing or sale of the property.

## Costs to Repair Property for Resale

Real estate purchase contracts that require repairs or maintenance to the property that the property owner cannot afford to complete must be explained. Two written bids must be submitted with the agreement to Fannie Mae for inclusion in the short-sale. These repairs may be presented to and negotiated with the servicing lender and the homeowner's insurance company.

## Repaired Value

The repaired value gives the lender the ability to estimate if it would be worth it for the lender to foreclose, repair the property, and put in on the market. A lender would consider doing this if it felt it would be able to recoup the defaulted mortgage, the back payments, the foreclosure costs, and the repair costs from the proceeds of a sale.

## Cost of Securing and Maintaining Property

A lender will estimate the cost of securing and maintaining a property that it may take back in a foreclosure sale. Securing a property includes protecting it from vandalism, repairing broken doors and windows, and turning on the water and utilities.

Maintaining a property includes removing rubbish and debris, mowing the lawn and taking care of the landscaping, watering, and keeping a pool or spa in good operating order. Securing and maintaining a property is necessary to be able to market the property effectively and receive the highest price.

## Cost of Holding and Selling Property

A lender will estimate the cost of holding and selling a property that it takes back in a foreclosure sale. Holding the property includes making necessary repairs, painting, and replacing damaged or broken built-in appliances, water heaters, heating and air conditioning units, carpeting and floor coverings.

Selling the property involves signing a listing agreement with a real estate broker, paying a real estate commission, and waiting four to six months or longer to find a buyer and close escrow. In addition to water and utility costs, the lender will also be responsible for property taxes, hazard insurance, and homeowners association dues, if any, through the selling period.

Understanding the 12 short-sale lender factors increases the likelihood that your short-sale offer will be well-received by the lender. The purpose of your real estate contract is to communicate. By demonstrating an understanding of short-sales from the lender's point of view, your short-sale offer presents solutions to the lender's problems.

In the next chapter we will show you how to write a short-sale offer. First of all, you must be in contact with the property owner to make a short-sale deal. You cannot approach the lender directly without the owner's permission. The property owner must accept your short-sale offer and agree to cooperate with you to get the lender to participate.

# CHAPTER 6

# Your Short-Sale Offer

There are no oral agreements in real estate. Everything must be in writing. In this chapter we will show you how to write an offer that will get you a great short-sale deal and protect you from winding up in a lousy deal.

We will also show you how to present your short-sale offer to the property owner in such a way that the property owner will see the advantage in accepting your offer. Remember, you have to be in contact with the property owner to make a short-sale deal. You cannot go directly to the lender without the owner's permission.

## Writing Your Short-Sale Offer

As we have said, there are no oral agreements in real estate. Yes, technically, you can agree to buy someone's property, and they can agree to sell it to you without a written agreement. However, if a dispute arises between you and the property owner and you wind up in front of the judge, the case will be thrown out of court as soon as the judge discovers there is no written agreement.

## Statute of Frauds

In the United States, every state has a statute of frauds that says that in order for a real estate contract to be valid it must be in writing. If the real estate contract is not in writing, the real estate contract cannot be enforced in a court of law. If the contract cannot be enforced, the contract is not valid. If the contract is not valid, there is no contract. You get the picture.

## Requirements of a Valid Contract

In addition to being written, a valid real estate contract must meet four other requirements. We call this the CoCa CoLa test. We are not promoting or advertising a soft drink here but using CoCa CoLa as a memory aid.

Once you understand these additional four requirements for a valid real estate contract you will always use the CoCa CoLa test to make sure all the requirements are present in your real estate contracts. These requirements are consent, capacity, consideration, and lawful object.

### *CoCa CoLa*

Consent: There must be mutual consent between the parties to the real estate contract. The parties to a real estate contract are typically the property owner and the buyer. We will find that the lender becomes a third party to a short-sale real estate contract. The parties have to agree (consent) to the wording and conditions written in the contract.

In a normal two-party real estate contract you, as the buyer, have only to sell the property owner on accepting your offer. In a short-sale transaction you, as the buyer, have to sell the property owner on accepting your offer. Then, after you have received the property owner's acceptance of your offer, you have to sell the real estate lender on accepting your short-sale offer.

Capacity: The parties to the real estate contract must have the capacity to enter into the contract. This means the parties have to be of sound mind (competent) and of legal age (18 in most places). There are some exceptions to the legal age requirement such as being married, or being married and then divorced, being in the military, or being an emancipated minor.

Consideration: Anything of value that influences a person to enter into a real estate contract is consideration. This could be money, a deed, a service, an item of personal property, an act (including the payment of money), or a promise (including the promise to pay on a loan). If the consideration is an act or a service, that act or service must be performed after the parties enter into the real estate contract.

Usually a buyer will attach some form of earnest money to the real estate contract to satisfy the consideration requirement. This can be in the form of cash (we don't recommend cash), a check, a money order, or a promissory note.

We recommend the use of a promissory note for two reasons. First, by using a promissory note you protect your cash. Second, you don't have 10, 15, or 20 personal checks out there accompanying all those short-sale offers you are writing and presenting. You only have to turn the promissory note into cash if your offer is accepted and you are going to open an escrow.

Lawful: Real estate is lawful for people to buy and sell. For a real estate contract to be valid the promises made between the parties must be legal. Also, the consideration given by the buyer must be legal to give. Now that you know the requirements of a valid contract, let's look into the various types of real estate contracts.

## Types of Real Estate Contracts

There are many types of real estate contracts. The purpose of any real estate contract is to communicate. We believe that the simpler the real estate contract the better the communication between the parties to the contract. You could write a real estate contract on the back of a napkin sitting in a restaurant. We've done it. Unfortunately, the napkin got wet from moisture on the table and the ink blurred. Our contract was illegible. Better to use regular paper instead.

When we first got into the real estate business we used a four-page real estate purchase contract in California. We heard tell from the grizzled old real estate veterans that when they first got in the business, they used a one-page real estate purchase contract!

This contract was basically a blank piece of paper. You made up your offer as you wrote it down. Talk about a simple real estate contract that would facilitate communication between the property owner and the buyer! What kind of a real estate contract should you use for your short-sale offers? We recommend you use a regionally standardized real estate purchase contract for your short-sale offers.

### Real Estate Purchase Contract

A real estate purchase contract is the basic agreement between you and the property owner for purchasing his property. Many variations of real estate purchase contracts exist. You can check with local Realtors, title insurance companies, or office supply stores to obtain a copy of the type of real estate purchase contract used in your area.

For example, in Texas, the Texas Real Estate Commission (TREC) provides a standard real estate purchase contract that must be used by all real estate licensees in Texas. However, the TREC real estate purchase contracts can be used both by non-licensees and real estate investors to make offers. You can download TREC real estate contracts from its web site at www.trec.state.tx.us. For those not in Texas you can look online for contracts available for your region.

Remember, regardless of the type of real estate purchase contract you use, the purpose of the contract is to communicate. The more straightforwardly the real estate purchase contract states your intentions to the property owner, the easier it will be for the property owner to understand what you are trying to do.

If the property owner understands what you are trying to do with your offer, it is more likely he will be accept your offer. In other words, the simpler your real estate purchase contract is the better.

### Design

Real estate purchase contracts have been designed to have standard clauses known as the boilerplate, which are to be used for all types of transactions. The blank lines and spaces in the contract are for you to customize your particular deal.

Whatever real estate purchase contract you are using, you begin to write by just filling in the blanks of the contract. Every blank space is either filled in, or the letters NA (not applicable) are written in. Many contracts begin with you filling in the city, state, and date. Then you fill in the name of the buyer (that's you!).

### *And/Or Assigns*

Now comes the exciting part! Before going any further into the contract, we are going to focus on the "Received from" or buyer's section. We are going to add three words to this line: and/or assigns. These are the three most powerful words you can have in a contract.

By adding and/or assigns to the buyer's name, we have created the opportunity for you to make money three ways rather than only one way. You can still make money the normal way by going ahead and buying the property yourself.

By adding and/or assigns you create a second way to make money. You can bring in a money partner to fund the transaction. You and assigns, the money partner, are now buying the property.

And/or assigns also gives you a third way to make money. You can assign the contract, you or assigns, for an assignment fee to another buyer. Now the other buyer is buying the property. You are not buying the property but assigning your interest in the purchase contract to another buyer and making money without buying or owning the property.

Assigning a contract is completely straightforward and legal. An assignment of a real estate purchase contract is designed to quickly provide a real estate solution for you and the property owner. Remember our adage that the purpose of the contract is to communicate. When a property owner asks you what and/or assigns means, this is what you should say:

**And/Or Assigns Script** "_____ (property owner's name), the and/or assigns clause gives both you and us the added flexibility of bringing in additional buyers or money partners to successfully close our transaction in a timely manner. Would that be all right with you?"

In our experience the property owner's answer has always been yes. Sometimes we have to work with a property owner for a while and educate him or her on the benefits that and/or assigns has for them.

What do you do if the property owner's answer is no? You want to make sure the property owner understands what you are trying to do by having the ability to assign your contract. Flexibility is the name of the game in making a real estate deal work.

This is especially true with a short-sale deal. If the property owner will not agree to give you the flexibility you need by having and/or assigns in your contract, let the property owner know that you will not proceed to present the rest of the contract.

You must stick to your guns on this point. And/or assigns is that important to your real estate investing success. It is much harder to come back to the negotiating table after you have already reached an agreement with the property owner. Have and/or assigns be part of your contract from the beginning.

A final note regarding and/or assigns. Due to the new lending laws you may find that you cannot assign your short-sale deal as readily as you could in the past. You may have to assign your accepted property owner short-sale contract before presenting it to the lender.

## *Financing*

A short-sale offer is an all-cash offer. There are no ifs, ands, or buts when you write a short-sale offer with regards to the financing. There is no financing. Cash is king. This is why after you have negotiated a good short-sale deal you may want to bring in a money partner to put up the cash to fund the deal. All of the net cash is going to the lender. Currently, the Federal Housing Administration (FHA) will allow only up to $1,000 going to the property owner.

A lender is willing to do a short-sale based on getting the short-sale price in cash. The short-sale lender typically will not refinance the loan it is going to short-sell. In the United States this may change over the course of 2009 and beyond as lenders work out the details and ramifications of the government bailout. Let's look at some numbers.

**Example**   Let's say the loan balance is $152,000. You present an offer to the property owner for $102,209. At the closing you and FHA agree to allow the property owner to receive $1,000. The short-sale lender will receive $101,209. The short-sale lender is taking a loss of more than $50,000. The short-sale lender will not agree to finance the $101,209.

| | |
|---|---:|
| Loan balance | $152,000 |
| Short-sale offer | 102,209 |
| Property owner receives | −1,000 |
| Lender receives | $101,209 |

After you have written your short-sale offer you have to present your short-sale offer. Remember, this real estate contract is a three-party contract. The three parties are the property owner, you, and the short-sale lender. You must first present your short-sale offer to the property owner. Once the property owner accepts your offer, then you present it to the lender.

## Presenting Your Offer

We are going to give you a crash course in real estate offer presentation. The purpose of presenting your offer is to have the property owner accept your short-sale offer. By building rapport with the property owner you dramatically increase the likelihood that the property owner will, eventually, accept your offer. This is referred to as a win-win tactic.

We have said that you communicate best when there is a rapport between you and the property owner. The reason you want to build a rapport with the property owner is to create a relationship between you and the property owner. A relationship means a good deal for everyone. No relationship means no deal for anyone.

## Building Rapport

You begin to build rapport the moment you start an interaction with a person. We have found that sincere smiles, respectfulness, and genuine interest in a property owner's situation build rapport. An encouraging and upbeat manner will instill confidence in the property owner that you can get a real estate transaction done.

We go into every interaction with a property owner with a win-win attitude. We want the property owner to win and we want to win. You will find as a real estate investor that getting a good deal is easy. You just have to ask. When we make an offer we want to get a good deal. And we find that when we get a good deal we are solving a problem for the property owner. That makes it win-win for us and the property owner.

## Where to Present Your Offer

We recommend presenting your offer in person. This is the most effective way to present an offer. We do not recommend presenting your offer over the phone. Presenting an offer by fax or by e-mail is less effective still.

Always present your offer at the seller's kitchen table. Arrange to sit at the head of the table with your back to an outside wall. You want the seller's attention focused on you and not what is going on in the rest of the house.

By presenting your offer at the kitchen table you convey that this is a business situation. If you present the offer in the living room it conveys a social interaction. Ask that the television and radio be turned off. Do not accept an offer of food. Accepting an offer of a beverage (nonalcoholic) is fine.

Keep the chitchat to no more than five minutes. At the appropriate time (see accompanying script) you will give the seller a copy of your offer so he can follow along with your presentation. You *are* going to make a presentation!

## When to Present Your Offer

Present your offer within 72 hours of seeing a property for the first time. There are two reasons for this. The first reason has to do with you. The second reason has to do with the property owner. We want you to present offers within 72 hours of seeing the property for the first time so you will present offers rather than procrastinate.

It gets very easy to find properties, look at the properties, get scared and not write and present offers, find more properties, look at properties, get scared.

Get the point? You will not make any money as a real estate investor unless you write *and* present offers. Remember: Do it now, not later! Be bold!

### *Within 72 Hours*

The reason we want you to present offers within 72 hours of seeing the property for the first time is so you will convey a sense of urgency and interest to the property owner. Property owners want to know that you are a serious buyer. Serious buyers take action in a timely manner. That is why it says on most real estate contracts, "Time is of the essence."

## How to Present Your Offer

We want to give you a script to use when you are presenting offers. The script is the same no matter what kind of real estate contract you are presenting. This may seem too simple for those of you who are experienced investors. If you have something that works for you, then by all means use it.

Practice the script in the mirror at home or with your real estate investment partner before you try it for real with a property owner. After the five minutes of chitchat at the property owner's kitchen table, this is what you say and do.

### *Script*

Pull out of your briefcase or folder two copies of your offer. Place them face down on the table in front of you. Look at the seller and say:

**"Mr. and Mrs. Property Owner** (if you are on a first name basis use the property owner's first name(s), **We are so excited to be able to present our offer to purchase your property today** (tonight)." Pause for the property owner's response.

**"Thank you for allowing us to come into your home."** Pause and smile.

**"As you know, we are real estate investors."** Pause. **"Our offer is designed to solve your real estate problems."** Pause. **"We want to do business with you."** Pause and nod your head up and down.

**"Before we go over the offer, we just want to make sure you still want to sell your property. Do you still want to sell your property?"** Pause and wait for first "yes."

**"Are you ready to go over the offer?"** Pause and wait for second "yes."

Turn over the two copies of your offer, which should be facing you and appear upside down or sideways to the property owner. Do not give the property owner his copy yet.

**"If we can solve your real estate problems, can we do business?"** Pause and wait for the third "yes".

Now give the property owner a copy of the offer.

## Three Responses

There are three responses a property owner can have to your short-sale offer. The property owner can accept your offer, counter your offer, or reject your offer. If the property owner accepts your short-sale offer you have a contract to take to the lender. If the property owner counters your short-sale offer you have something to work with. If the property owner rejects your short-sale offer, you may be at a dead end. Obviously, you don't want the property owner to say no.

## You Must Make Money

You cannot help the property owner solve his real estate problems without making money for yourself. You are a real estate investor not a real estate philanthropist. Do not buy the property owner's problems.

The purpose of the script is to make property owner receptive to your offer. If the property owner does not accept your offer, talk over the sticking points and ask the property owner for a counteroffer.

Know what you and your money partners are prepared to do before you accept a counteroffer from the property owner. We have found that we can create a win-win for us and the property owner by using the script. Be yourself and stick with the script!

In the next chapter we will show you what to do after you have reached a meeting of the minds with the property owner. Next on the agenda is getting your accepted short-sale offer to the decision maker for the lender. Once you get the lender to accept your short-sale offer, you have to close the transaction.

# CHAPTER 7

# Presenting Your Short-Sale Offer and Closing the Transaction

Next on the agenda is getting your accepted short-sale offer presented to the real estate lender. Once the lender has received your short-sale offer, negotiations are game on. After you get the lender to accept your short-sale offer, you have to close the transaction.

Hopefully, you have established a rapport with the person who works in the lender's loss mitigation department who has the authority to make a deal for the property you are interested in purchasing. You may think you have a deal worked out over the phone. However, as with all real estate investments, everything must be in writing to be valid.

After you have made a deal with the property owner to do a short-sale, had the property owner give you written authorization to make contact with the lender, obtained a financial hardship letter from the property owner, assembled supporting documentation, and written a purchase contract that is signed by you and the property owner, you are ready to submit your short-sale offer to the lender.

Each lender has its own preferred method of processing short-sale offers. You may be able to submit your sales contract and supporting documentation to the lender by facsimile. Some lenders will allow you to submit your offer to them by e-mail using attachments. You may have to FedEx or mail a hardcopy of the paperwork to the lender. Once you have the paperwork into the lenders hands you will be able to proceed with the possibility of negotiations.

## Negotiating with the Lender

With foreclosure looming the lender is about to become the property owner.

In a crashing real estate market, there is not enough equity to attract a real estate investor offering more than the lender's credit bid by the time the foreclosure sale occurs.

We said in Chapter 4 that we would revisit our short-sale example and present our negotiations with the lender. Remember we found an owner who was four months behind on his $3,200 monthly mortgage payment for a total of $12,800.

The amount outstanding on the loan was $600,000. The lender was about to foreclose. The lender would like to receive the $600,000 loan balance plus $12,800 for the four back payments.

### Lender Desired Payoff

| | |
|---|---|
| Loan balance | $600,000 |
| Back payments | +12,800 |
| Lender's desired payoff | $612,800 |

The property was worth $510,000. The owner was underwater $102,800.

### Owner Underwater

| | |
|---|---|
| Property value | $510,000 |
| Lender's desired payoff | −612,800 |
| Owner underwater | −$102,800 |

## Our Offer

We offered the lender $439,000 and the lender accepted our offer. Why did the lender accept our $439,000 loan payoff offer? Because it was in the lender's best interest to do so! If the lender went through the foreclosure process and no one bid at the foreclosure sale because it looked like there was no equity in the property, the lender would still have all the foreclosure costs.

### *Foreclosure Costs: $9,000*

These costs include posting a notice of foreclosure and advertising the foreclosure sale. The lender would have to pay attorney's fees and trustee's fees as well as foreclosure sale expenses. The lender would also have to pay for title insurance. The list goes on. The total could easily be $8,000 to $9,000.

### *Holding Costs: $6,000*

After the lender took back the property it would have additional expenses. The lender would have to pay for repairs and fix-up costs, ongoing maintenance, hazard insurance, property taxes, and human resources costs. Let's call these costs holding costs. Again, the list goes on. This could easily amount to another $5,000 to $6,000.

### *Closing Costs and Commissions: $40,000*

And finally, the lender would have to put the property on the market for sale. The lender would have the closing costs and real estate commissions to pay in the same range as the seller. This is an additional $35,000 to $40,000!

The lender was hoping to receive $612,800. The property had dropped in value to $510,000. Assume the lender received this amount from the sale of the property. What would the lender net after all costs?

**Lender's Net**

| | |
|---|---|
| Lender payoff | $510,000 |
| Foreclosure costs | 9,000 |
| Holding costs | 6,000 |
| Closing costs & commissions | −40,000 |
| Lender's net | $455,000 |

Our offer of $439,000 now looked very attractive to the lender. The lender would not have to conduct a foreclosure sale. Plus it would not have to wait six to nine months for the property to sell if no one buys the property at the foreclosure sale. The lender would also avoid having the holding costs and paying the closing costs and real estate commissions. This became a win-win-win deal for Mr. O'Rourke, the lender, and us.

## Our Profit

So how did we make out on this deal? We had an instant equity position of $71,000.

**Our Equity**

| | |
|---|---|
| Property value | $510,000 |
| Negotiated lender payoff | −439,000 |
| Our equity | $ 71,000 |

Within two weeks, we sold this property for $510,000. We will tell you how we did it in Chapter 9: Sellers Are the New Bankers.

## The Nine Steps to a Successful Short-Sale

As a final synopsis for putting together a successful short-sale we give you the nine steps to a successful short-sale.

**The Nine Steps to a Successful Short-Sale**

1. Finding property owners in distress.
2. Making a deal with the property owner to do a short-sale.
3. Written authorization to make contact with the lender.
4. Obtaining a financial hardship letter.
5. Assembling supporting documentation.
6. Writing a purchase contract.
7. Submitting your short-sale offer to the lender.
8. Negotiating with the lender.
9. Closing your short-sale deal.

## Closing Your Short-Sale Deal

The last step in a successful short-sale deal is closing the transaction. This means you give the lender the agreed upon short-sale loan payoff.

The lender signs off on the mortgage loan removing the security interest the lender has against the title.

The property owner signs a deed giving you title to the property. The title insurance company ensures that you are receiving clear title. Without the transfer of ownership from the property owner to you, there may not be much profit for you in the deal. A transfer of ownership revolves around escrow, closing, and title insurance.

# Escrow

Escrow is a type of closing by which you and the property owner deposit money and/or documents with a neutral third party—the escrow holder. Whoever handles the closing of your real estate short-sale acts as an agent for you and the property owner.

You and the property owner give the escrow holder instructions to hold and disburse documents and funds after certain conditions are met. The escrow holder acts as an impartial stakeholder and communicates with everyone involved in the transaction.

We recommend having an escrow because of the complexity of the closing process. The advantages of escrow are that the escrow holder is responsible for keeping documents and funds safe, making computations, receiving and distributing funds, carrying out the terms of the real estate contract, complying with regional, federal, state, and local tax regulations, providing an accounting for the transfer process, and determining that all conditions have been satisfied.

## *Escrow Is Complete*

An escrow is complete when all conditions listed in the escrow instructions are met and all acts specified in the instructions are performed. When an escrow is complete, the escrow holder disburses the funds and documents to close the escrow.

In its simplest format, an escrow would have the buyer put the money in the escrow account at the opening of the escrow. The seller would take the money out of the escrow at the closing of the escrow. The seller would put the deed to the property in escrow at the opening of the escrow. The buyer would take the deed to the property out of the escrow at the closing of the escrow.

### What Occurs in Escrow

Many things are occurring during the escrow period: termite inspections, physical inspections, money partner inspections, geological inspections, title searches, procuring hazard insurance, obtaining financing, preparing loan documents, calculating closing costs, preparing deeds, and so on.

Escrow holders are usually prohibited from offering advice, negotiating with you and the property owner, revealing information about the escrow to people who are not a party to the escrow, and preparing or revising escrow instructions without the authorization of you and the property owner. So how do you open an escrow?

### Opening an Escrow

Consider choosing an escrow holder who is willing to take the time to explain what is happening and what you need to do. Choose a company that is located a convenient distance from where you live or work so you can deliver and sign documents or deliver money easily.

Depending on your area, the party that acts as the escrow holder can include independent escrow companies, escrow departments of lending institutions, title insurance companies, real estate brokers, real estate attorneys, and in some places, trustees. You may find that your area does a closing with an attorney rather than conducting an escrow.

After you select an escrow holder, open the escrow by following these steps:

1.  Contact the escrow holder by telephone or in person.
2.  Give the escrow holder all the relevant information regarding the sale.
3.  Deposit the earnest money with the escrow holder, preferably in person or if necessary by certified mail.

### Escrow Officer Collects Information

The escrow officer collects the information necessary to prepare escrow instructions on a form that is sometimes called a "take sheet." Data the escrow holder may need in order to prepare escrow instructions include the following nine items:

1.  Property description.
2.  Parties to the transaction.
3.  Proposed closing date.
4.  Sales price.
5.  Loans currently on the property. (This is important in a short-sale.)
6.  Loans buyer wants to put on the property.
7.  Vesting of the title in the new owner.
8.  Conditions of the title such as covenants and restrictions.
9.  Buyers' and sellers' costs.

So what are escrow instructions about?

## Escrow Instructions

Escrow instructions are the written agreement between you and the property owner that translates the real estate contract into a form used by the escrow holder to conduct and close the escrow. The escrow holder prepares the escrow instructions, using the take sheet as a guideline, so that the intent and conditions are identical to those in the contract. The escrow holder then asks you and the owner to read and sign the escrow instructions.

## Read the Escrow Instructions Carefully

You should read the escrow instructions carefully. Make sure that the intent and conditions of the escrow instructions are identical to those in the purchase contract. Ask questions about items you do not understand or ones that do not appear to match those in the contract. Sign the escrow instructions only when you are satisfied that all items reflect exactly the terms of the purchase contract.

You and the property owner can make amendments to the escrow instructions. To make an amendment, discuss the changes with the owner and obtain his agreement to make the change. Request that the escrow holder prepare documents for the change and send these documents to you and the owner. Sign the documents authorizing the change (the owner must also sign) and return the documents to the escrow holder. Now you are ready to close.

## Closing

Understanding how the escrow closes can make you comfortable with a process many buyers and sellers find very confusing. Closing is the process in which funds and property title are transferred between you and the property owner.

Although closing could be accomplished by you and the property owner simply getting together and exchanging money and documents, most real estate transactions today use an escrow type of closing. So how are prorations handled?

### The Buyer's Day

The day the escrow closes is considered the buyer's day. What this means is that all the prorations of property taxes, hazard insurance, mortgage interest, and property rents are figured on this day. Prorations are the apportionment of charges owed on the property between the seller and the buyer.

Let's say the escrow closes on the 14th day of the month. The seller is responsible for paying the property taxes, hazard insurance, and mortgage interest through the 13th day of the month. If the property is receiving rental income, the seller is entitled to receive a prorated share of the monthly rent through the 13th day of the month. This is because rents are paid in advance, usually on the first day of the month.

The buyer is responsible for paying the property taxes, hazard insurance, and mortgage interest starting on the 14th day of the month. If the property is receiving rental income, the buyer is entitled to receive a prorated share of the monthly rent from the 14th day of the month until the end of the month.

### Short-Sale Closing

We recommend you find an escrow holder who is adept at handling short-sale closings. It becomes very important if you are using the same escrow holder to handle the buying portion of the short-sale property and the immediate selling portion of the short-sale property. In other words if you are immediately flipping your short-sale, the escrow holder has to do it right.

We know of a situation where the escrow holder made the egregious error of telling the short-sale lender about the new lender financing the property for $45,000 more than the short-sale lender was receiving. Needless to say there was hell to pay. People lost their jobs and the investor lost the short-sale deal.

### *Closing Statement*

Once the escrow closes, a closing statement is prepared by the escrow holder. In the United States all closing statements are referred to as a HUD 1. HUD stands for the Department of Housing and Urban Development.

We have our escrow holder prepare an estimated HUD 1 to submit with our short-sale offer to the lender. That way the lender can see how much money it will receive at the closing as a result of accepting our short-sale offer.

The closing statement is set up as a debit and credit accounting. The purchase price appears as a credit to the seller and a debit to the buyer. Any rental security deposits will be credited to the buyer and debited to the seller. Everything else will be prorated as a debit and a credit to the seller and buyer, respectively, based on the day of closing. Let's talk about title insurance next.

## Title Insurance

If you buy property, get title insurance. *Never buy property without title insurance.* What is title insurance? Title insurance is a policy of insurance issued to you by a title company on completion of the final title search, which protects your title to property against claims made in the future based on circumstances in the past.

Title insurance is especially important when you are investing in foreclosures. Liens and encumbrances against the property title tend to mushroom during the foreclosure process. Besides the foreclosing lender there may be tax liens, lawsuits, and other creditors with interests against the title to the property.

## Exceptions

There are exceptions to our rule regarding buying title insurance. We know of an investor who bids on properties on the courthouse steps and does no preliminary research on either the condition of the title or the property. After he wins a bid, he goes inside the courthouse and checks the condition of the title using the public records. At the same time he has a partner do a drive-by inspection of the property.

He takes advantage of the two-hour window the foreclosing trustee allows for the winning bidder to produce the cash or cashier's checks. If the property looks like a bomb (not *the bomb*), he backs out of the deal. If he discovers problems with the title to the property too great for him to handle, he backs out of the deal.

Any problems too great to handle with the title to the property are easily discovered through a title search.

## Title Search

A title search is an examination of information recorded on a property, or the owner of the property, at the county recorder's office in the county where the property is located. The examination verifies that the property will have no outstanding liens or claims against it to adversely affect a buyer or lender when the title to the property is transferred to a new buyer or pledged as collateral for a real estate loan.

## Preliminary Report

When you are buying property, especially in a short-sale situation, it is always a good idea to get a preliminary title report from a title insurance company. The preliminary title report is usually produced by the title company during the escrow or closing.

The purpose of the preliminary report is to make everyone—buyer, seller, lender, escrow holder, title company—aware of the condition of the title involved in the transaction. Let's talk briefly about the types of title policies. These types of title policies include the owner's policy, buyer's policy, and lender's policy.

### Owner's Policy

An owner's policy of title insurance protects the owner of record from claims against the title brought by other parties. If a claim arises and you have title insurance and any monetary damages are to be paid, the title insurance company will pay them. By the way, the seller or buyer can pay for the owner's policy. You want to get the owner's policy of title insurance on all your short-sale deals. This will protect your great short-sale investment from potential disaster.

### Buyer's Policy

A buyer's policy of title insurance protects the buyer of real estate. The buyer's policy is similar to the lender's policy in that it protects the buyer in matters beyond what is in the public record. Although the buyer becomes the owner and is protected by the owner's policy, a buyer may feel he wants extended coverage. We recommend getting buyer's coverage any time you are involved in a foreclosure transaction.

### Lender's Policy

A lender's policy of title insurance protects the real estate lender beyond matters of public record. There may be unrecorded liens against the title. A lender wants to be protected against everything because it has so much money loaned on the property. Typically, the lender requires the buyer who is using the loan proceeds to complete the purchase of the property to pay for the lender's title policy.

So now you have closed a short-sale transaction with a lender. What if you do not want to actually have a property to hold or flip or you do not want to bother with the seller at this juncture? In the next chapter we will show you how to buy a mortgage in foreclosure from the lender. It is possible to talk to the real estate lender without the property owner's permission if you are interested in buying the mortgage paper held by the lender.

You buy the lender's position in the mortgage note for a substantial discount from the face value amount. In essence you are making a short-sale deal with the lender. If you make a successful deal to buy the mortgage in foreclosure from the lender you can make money three ways. These three ways are covered in the next chapter.

# CHAPTER 8

# Buying the Mortgage in Foreclosure

You have the opportunity to make a significant amount of money by purchasing the mortgage from a lender before the foreclosure sale. You buy the lender's position in the mortgage note for a substantial discount on the face amount. In essence, you are making a short-sale deal with the lender.

You also do not need the borrower/owner's permission to talk to the lender. You are approaching the lender directly and asking if it would be interested in selling the mortgage. Lenders sell their mortgages all the time and borrowers do not even know about it until the next time they get something from their lender in the mail.

Buying a mortgage in foreclosure gives you three ways to make money. The first way you can make money is if the borrower makes up the default. This will give you a tremendous yield on your investment as the holder of the note.

The second way you can make money is to continue the foreclosure process on the defaulting borrower. If no one outbids your credit bid at the foreclosure sale you will wind up owning the property that is the security for the mortgage note.

Finally, the third way you can make money is if someone bids above your credit bid at the foreclosure sale. Then they have to pay you off in cash. So how do you negotiate to buy a mortgage in foreclosure from the lender?

## Real Estate Paperwork

Before we talk about negotiating with the lender, we need to give you some information on how real estate title-to-property and real estate financing-of-property interact. This is the paperwork of real estate. Once you have this information you will better understand real estate lenders' perspectives and how best to approach buying the mortgage in foreclosure.

There are three aspects to the title and lending paperwork. First, there is the paperwork involved on the title side. Second, there is the paperwork involved on the financing side. Finally, there is the paperwork bridging the title side and the financing side known as the security side. Let's start with the title side.

## Title Side

Using the United State for example, on the title side there are two types of deeds used to convey the property title from one owner to the next. These two deeds are grant deeds and warranty deeds. Check with your local tile conveyance official or law agent specializing in title conveyance.

### Grant Deed

A *grant deed* is a deed using the word grant in the clause that awards ownership. This document is used by the grantor (seller) to transfer the title of his property to the grantee (buyer). Grant deeds have two implied warranties. One is that the grantor has not previously transferred the title. The second is that the title is free from encumbrances that are not visible to the grantee. This deed also transfers title acquired after delivery of the deed from the seller to the buyer. Delivery means the seller has signed the deed and deposited the deed in escrow.

### Warranty Deed

A *warranty deed* is a deed in which the grantor (usually the seller) guarantees the title to the property to be in the condition indicated in the deed. The grantor agrees to protect the grantee (usually the buyer) against all claims to the property made by anyone other than holders of recorded liens (matters of record). A warranty deed gives a warranty to the title holder.

**Title Side**

| Grant Deed | | Warranty Deed | |
|---|---|---|---|
| Grantor (Seller) Or (Owner) | Grantee (Buyer) | Grantor (Seller) Or (Owner) | Grantee (Buyer) |

Now let's discuss the financing side.

## Financing Side

The paperwork involved on the financing side is the evidence of the debt. The two types of paperwork that are used as evidence of the debt are the promissory note and the mortgage note. This paperwork is used by lenders and borrowers to create a written agreement about the terms and conditions for the real estate loan.

### *Promissory Note*

A *promissory note* is the written contract a borrower signs promising to pay back a definite amount of money by a definite future date to a lender. A promissory note has four basic elements. These are the amount of the note, the interest rate of the note, the term of the note, and the payments, if any, on the note. A promissory note that has no payments till the due date of the note is called a straight note.112

### *Mortgage Note*

A *mortgage note* is a written contract signed by a borrower in which the borrower agrees to pay back a lender the amount of money the lender loaned the borrower. Similar to a promissory note, a mortgage note specifies the amount of the note, the interest rate of the note, the term of the note, and the payments on the note.

### Financing Side

| Promissory Note | | Mortgage Note | |
|---|---|---|---|
| Borrower (maker of the note) | Lender (holder of the note) | Borrower (maker of the note) | Lender (holder of the note) |

Finally let's talk about the bridge between the title side and the financing side known as the security side.

## Security Side

The paperwork involved on the security side is trust deeds and mortgage contracts. They are regarded as security devices for the promissory notes and mortgage notes, respectively. Another way to say this is that the trust deed and mortgage contracts are the collateral for the lender in the event a borrower defaults on the loan. They become liens against the property title when they are officially recorded at the county recorder's office in the county where the property that is the security or collateral for the lien is located.

### Trust Deed

A *trust deed* is a document, used as a security device for a loan on a property, by which the owner transfers bare (naked) legal title with the power of sale to a trustee. This transfer is in effect until the owner totally pays off the loan.

There are three parties to a trust deed. These three parties are the trustor, the trustee, and the beneficiary. The trustor is the owner/borrower who transfers the bare legal title with a power of sale to the trustee. The trustee is a person who holds the bare legal title to a property without being the actual owner of the property. The trustee has the power of sale for the lender's benefit. The beneficiary is the lender of money on a property used in a trust deed type of loan.

## Trust Deed

| | | |
|---|---|---|
| 1 Trustor<br>(Borrower) | | 2 Trustee<br>(Power of sale) |
| | 3 Beneficiary<br>(Lender) | |

### *Mortgage Contract*

A *mortgage contract* is a document, used as a security device for a loan on a property, by which the owner/borrower promises his property as security or collateral without giving up possession of or title to the property.

There are two parties to a mortgage contract. These two parties are the mortgagor and the mortgagee. The mortgagor is the owner/borrower who uses a mortgage contract to borrow money. The mortgagee is the lender of money on a property used in a mortgage-contract-type of loan.

## Mortgage Contract

| 1<br>Mortgagor<br>(Borrower) | 2<br>Mortgagee<br>(Lender) |
|---|---|

## What It All Means

Foreclosure is possible because of the paperwork of real estate. The relationship of the title paperwork, the financing paperwork, and the security paperwork gives the lender the ability to protect its interest in a property when it loans money to a borrower.

The security paperwork, trust deeds, and mortgages, form the bridge between the ownership, or title, side and the finance side. The promissory notes and mortgage notes create the security devices that become liens against the title to the property.

Once you understand the paperwork of real estate you will be able to negotiate on an equal footing with real estate lenders. This is especially important when you are negotiating with lenders in the short-sale arena.

All this paperwork comes down to contracts. All contracts come down to what does the paperwork say? When you understand what the paperwork says, then you can control what happens to property. This next illustration helps clarify the paperwork relationships.

### The Paperwork

| <u>Title</u> | <u>Security Devices</u> | <u>Finance</u> |
|---|---|---|
| Grant Deed or Warranty Deed Grantor / Grantee (Seller) / (Buyer) | Trust Deed Trustor / Trustee Beneficiary (Lender) | Promissory Note |
| | Mortgage Contract Mortgagor / Mortgagee (Borrower) / (Lender) | Mortgage Note |

Now that you understand the title and financing paperwork and the corresponding security devices for them, we can move on to negotiating with the lender.

## Negotiating with the Lender

To get started we recommend you look for lenders that are private party lenders with limited experience in foreclosing on a mortgage note. This is usually the case when the mortgage note holder is an out-of-the-area private party. These lenders are often unaware of the foreclosure process in your area.

They tend to have more motivation to sell than a local or professional note holder (commercial lender). We do think in the near future commercial lenders, as part of the United States government bailout, will participate in selling their mortgage notes at short-sale prices to help alleviate the pressure of their nonperforming loans.

## Preparation

When you are contacting lenders, it is very important that you are well prepared to discuss the foreclosure situation. You should be able to make a presentation with as many specifics as possible. You need to know the details of the foreclosure procedure, the risks to the lender, and the options to minimize risks to the lender. In other words, proceed as if you were putting together a short-sale offer.

Obtain as much preliminary information as you can prior to the meeting. This should include copies of the notice of default, a property profile, and a report on taxes paid. The notice of default will be posted at your county courthouse. A title company may provide you property profiles and tax information. Take pictures of the property. Various shooting angles may be helpful in demonstrating to the lender that the property may have more risk than desirable to the lender.

Complete a market analysis using comparable sales that have closed no longer than three months prior to your lender appointment. Include questions for the lender to answer at the scheduled meeting time.

### Questions for Private Party Lenders

- Are you aware of the foreclosure proceeding?
- Do you know what you will have to do to protect your interest?
- Do you have the resources to maintain the payments on the senior loans?
- Are you willing to take the time and make the effort to foreclose?
- Would you accept cash now rather than possibly nothing in the future?

Be certain to itemize the cost to repair and improve the property to saleable standards. Include the cost for holding and marketing the property. Put together a presentation book that includes all of the above and use it as a guide at the meeting with the lender.

Before you offer to purchase a mortgage note, you should be certain that your evaluation of the property indicates that it is a smart investment. Also you should always anticipate that the borrower may file for bankruptcy protection and stay the foreclosure (stay is the legal term a court uses to halt foreclosure temporarily).

## Three Ways to Make Money

We said earlier that there are three ways to make money. The first way is to buy the mortgage note for a short-sale price and the borrower makes up the default. The second way you can make money is to continue the foreclosure process on the defaulting borrower and possibly end up owning the property. The third way you can make money is if someone bids above your credit bid at the foreclosure sale.

### *Buy the Note and the Borrower Makes Up the Default*

Let's create an example we can use for all three ways to make money. You find a holder of a first mortgage with an initial balance of $100,000. The interest rate is 8 percent annually. The loan is amortized for 30 years with a balloon payment due after 5 years. The monthly payment of principal and interest is $734.

#### Loan Terms

| | |
|---|---|
| Note amount | $100,000 |
| Interest rate | 8% |
| Loan term | 30 years |
| Monthly payment | $   734 |

The borrower makes payments for two years and gets three payments behind. The lender files a notice of default. The property is worth $115,000.

You approach the lender and make a short-sale offer to buy the note at a discount. You offer the lender $78,000 for the note. This is a $20,260 or a 21 percent discount from the remaining balance of $98,260.

#### Dollar Discount

| | |
|---|---|
| Remaining balance | $98,260 |
| Your offer | −78,000 |
| Dollar discount | $20,260 |

#### Percentage Discount

$$\frac{\$20,260}{\$98,260} = 21\%$$

The lender accepts your offer. You step into the lender's shoes and continue the foreclosure process. The borrower is now four months behind for a total of $2,936.

#### Payments Behind

| | |
|---|---|
| Monthly payment | $  734 |
| Months behind | × 4 |
| Total behind | $2,936 |

The borrower contacts you before the foreclosure sale and wants to make up the back payments. You agree to reinstate the loan for the

$2,936. The borrower will resume making the regular monthly payment of $734.

There will be another 31 months of $734 payments for a total of $22,754. Then a final balloon payment of $95,804 is due. Let's see what kind of return you have received in less than three years. Remember you originally invested $78,000.

You initially received the four months of back payments to stop the foreclosure. This was $2,936. You then received 31 months of additional monthly payments. This was $22,754. Finally, you received a balloon payment. The balloon payment was $95,804. This is a total of $121,494.

### Total Received

| | |
|---|---|
| Back payments | $    2,936 |
| Monthly payments | 22,754 |
| Balloon payment | +95,804 |
| Total received | $121,494 |

A $121,494 return on a $78,000 investment is a $43,494 profit.

### Profit

| | |
|---|---|
| Total return | $121,494 |
| Amount invested | −78,000 |
| Profit | $  43,494 |

A $43,494 profit on a $78,000 investment is a 56 percent total return on your investment. That works!

### Total Return

$$\frac{\$43,494}{\$78,000} = 56\%$$

Figured on an annualized yield basis you made an 18 percent return on your $78,000 investment. We'll take it!

### Buy the Note and Foreclose on the Property

You buy the note from the lender at the short-sale price of $78,000. The borrower does nothing to make up the payments. You go through with the foreclosure sale.

At the foreclosure sale you make your credit bid for the remaining loan balance, plus the four months of no payments received, plus the foreclosure costs. The remaining loan balance is $98,260. The four monthly payments are $2,936. The foreclosure costs are $1,700. This is a total of $102,898.

### Credit Bid

| | |
|---|---:|
| Loan balance | $ 98,260 |
| Back payments | 2,936 |
| Foreclosure costs | +1,700 |
| Credit bid | $102,898 |

No one outbids your credit bid. Depending upon whether you are foreclosing on a mortgage note or a promissory note, you will receive a sheriff's deed or a trustee's deed to the property. You have now gone from being the lender on the property to the owner of the property.

We said the property is worth $115,000. You have your original $78,000 invested in buying the note. You have an additional $1,700 in foreclosure costs. You have a total invested in the property of less than $80,000.

### Invested in Property

| | |
|---|---:|
| Original investment | $78,000 |
| Foreclosure costs | +1,700 |
| Total invested | $79,700 |

You have an equity position of $35,300.

### Equity Position

| | |
|---|---:|
| Market value | $115,000 |
| Total invested | −79,700 |
| Equity position | $ 35,300 |

A $35,300 equity position on a $79,700 investment is a 44 percent return on your investment.

### Return on Investment

$$\frac{\$35,300}{\$79,700} = 44\%$$

Depending on whether your investment strategy is quick cash or longer term wealth building, you can sell or rent the property.

### *Buy the Note and Be Outbid at the Foreclosure Sale*

The third way to make money is to buy the note at a short-sale price, conduct the foreclosure sale, and have your credit bid outbid by another investor at the foreclosure sale. We said your credit bid would be made up of three parts. It would consist of the loan balance, the back payments, and your foreclosure costs.

**Credit Bid**

| | |
|---|---:|
| Loan balance | $ 98,260 |
| Back payments | 2,936 |
| Foreclosure costs | +1,700 |
| Credit bid | $102,898 |

Let's say someone bids $102,900. How do you make out? You have your original $78,000 investment plus your $1,700 in foreclosure costs for a total investment of $79,700.

**Invested in Property**

| | |
|---|---:|
| Original investment | $78,000 |
| Foreclosure costs | +1,700 |
| Total invested | $79,700 |

This means you have made $23,200 in 30 to 60 days.

**Profit**

| | |
|---|---:|
| Total return | $102,900 |
| Amount invested | −79,700 |
| Profit | $ 23,200 |

A $23,200 profit on a $79,700 investment is a 29 percent total return on your investment.

**Total Return**

$$\frac{\$23,200}{\$79,700} = 29\%$$

Figured on an annualized yield basis you made a 174% return on your $79,700 investment if the foreclosure sale was 60 days after you bought the note. You made a 348% return on your $79,700 investment if the foreclosure sale was 30 days after you bought the note. Now what do you think about buying a mortgage note at a short-sale price?

In the next chapter we begin Part Two. In Part Two we present what you must do over the next four years to become multimillionaires investing in real estate. This starts with understanding that in a crashing real estate market, sellers are the new bankers for real estate investors.

# PART TWO

# CHAPTER 9

# Sellers Are the New Bankers

In a crashing real estate market, sellers are the new bankers. Part of your job as a real estate investor is to educate sellers on their role as bankers in order to have your deal go through. Once you understand the benefit of the seller being the banker for your own deals, then you will find it easier to educate your sellers when you are the buyer.

In this chapter we want to give you the perspective of being in the position of selling a property and being the banker. You may be in a position to short-sale your own lending position so to speak and make an excellent return on your loan. This can happen even when real estate prices are declining.

## Being the Banker

Let's say you decide to sell one of your properties. The property is worth $250,000. You owe $150,000 on a first mortgage. You have a $100,000 equity position in this property.

### Your Equity

| | |
|---|---|
| Property value | $250,000 |
| First mortgage | −150,000 |
| Your equity | $100,000 |

Let's say you sell this property for $250,000. The buyer assumes your $150,000 first mortgage. The buyer makes a $50,000 cash down payment. In order to complete the transaction, you agree to be the banker for the buyer and extend credit to him in the form of carrying a second mortgage. You carry a $50,000 mortgage note secured by a second mortgage on the property. You go from being an owner of the property to being a banker on the property.

### Being the Banker

| | |
|---|---|
| Assumed first mortgage | $150,000 |
| Carried second mortgage | 50,000 |
| Buyer's down payment | +50,000 |
| Sales price | $250,000 |

## Buyer Defaults

Two years go by. The property drops in value and is now worth $230,000. The buyer defaults on the first and second mortgages. You foreclose on your second mortgage. No one outbids your opening credit bid at the foreclosure sale. You get the property back subject to the first mortgage.

In essence you have made a short-sale to yourself on your second mortgage. The second mortgage has been extinguished by the foreclosure sale. All that remains on the property is the first mortgage.

### Foreclosed Second Mortgage

| | |
|---|---|
| First mortgage | $150,000 |
| Foreclosed second mortgage | + 0 |
| Total mortgages | $150,000 |

## Total Net Return

You go from being the banker on the property to owning the property again. You keep the original $50,000 down payment. You keep the two years worth of payments you have received on your second mortgage, which amounts to $12,000. You get the benefit of two years of principal reduction on the $150,000, now $147,000, first mortgage.

Let's say it cost you $9,000 to make up the back payments on the first mortgage plus pay the foreclosure expenses. How do you come out? As we said the property is now worth $230,000.

### Total Net Return

| | |
|---|---:|
| Property value now | $230,000 |
| First mortgage now | −147,000 |
| Your equity position | $ 83,000 |
| Cash down payment | 50,000 |
| Payments on second mortgage | +12,000 |
| Total return | $145,000 |
| Foreclosure expenses | −9,000 |
| Total net return | $136,000 |

It looks like you came out smelling like a rose. You can keep the property for long-term wealth building or you can immediately resell it for quick cash.

## *Resell It*

Let's say you resell the property for $230,000. The buyer assumes your $147,000 first mortgage. The buyer makes a $33,000 cash down payment. In order to complete the transaction, you agree to be the banker for the buyer in the form of carrying a second mortgage. You carry a $50,000 mortgage note secured by a second mortgage on the property. Again, you go from being an owner of the property to being the banker on the property.

### Being the Banker

| | |
|---|---:|
| Assumed first mortgage | $147,000 |
| Carried second mortgage | 50,000 |
| Buyer's down payment | +33,000 |
| Sales price | $230,000 |

## *Buyer Defaults*

Two years go by. The property drops in value and is now worth $200,000. The buyer defaults on the first and second mortgages. You foreclose on your second mortgage. No one outbids your opening credit bid at the foreclosure sale. You get the property back subject to the first mortgage.

The second mortgage has been extinguished by the foreclosure sale. All that remains on the property is the first mortgage.

### Foreclosed Second Mortgage

| | |
|---|---|
| First mortgage | $147,000 |
| Foreclosed second mortgage | + 0 |
| Total mortgages | $147,000 |

## *Total Net Return*

You go from being the banker on the property to owning the property again. You keep the original $30,000 down payment. You keep the two years worth of payments you have received on your second mortgage, which amounts to another $12,000. You get the benefit of two years of principal reduction on the $147,000, now $144,000, first mortgage.

Let's say it again cost you $9,000 to make up the back payments on the first mortgage plus pay the foreclosure expenses. How do you come out? As we said the property is now worth $200,000.

### Total Net Return

| | |
|---|---|
| Property value now | $200,000 |
| First mortgage now | −144,000 |
| Your equity position | $ 56,000 |
| Cash down payment | 33,000 |
| Payments on second mortgage | +$ 12,000 |
| Total return | $101,000 |
| Foreclosure expenses | −9,000 |
| Total net return | $ 92,000 |

By you, as the seller, being the banker you have made $228,000 in four years. You made $136,000 after two years. You made another $92,000 in the next two years. And this is occurring with the value of the property dropping from $250,000 to $200,000!

## Second Mortgage

We found a property that we felt was worth $250,000. The property owner agreed to sell us the property for $200,000. We were going to take over the owner's existing first mortgage of $150,000. What was left for us to figure out was how we were going to cover the $50,000 equity position the property owner had in the property.

### Owner Equity

| | |
|---|---|
| Purchase price | $200,000 |
| first mortgage | − 150,000 |
| Owner equity | $ 50,000 |

At first the owner insisted that he needed to receive all of his equity in cash. We wanted to put no more than $40,000 in cash into the deal. We wrote our offer to include a $40,000 cash down payment and asked the property owner to extend a $10,000 second mortgage.

We presented our offer for $200,000 with us taking over the existing $150,000 first mortgage, making a $40,000 cash down payment, and requesting the owner to carry back a $10,000 second mortgage.

### Our Offer

| | |
|---|---|
| Purchase price | $200,000 |
| Take over existing first mortgage | 150,000 |
| Cash down payment | $ 40,000 |
| Owner second mortgage | 10,000 |
| Owner receives | $ 50,000 |

During the offer presentation we educated the property owner on the benefits of carrying back a second mortgage. If the owner carried back the $10,000 at 7 percent annual interest payable $100 or more monthly all due in 36 months, he would receive $3,600 in monthly payments. After 36 months he would receive a $9,673 balloon payment. The total he would receive carrying the second mortgage would be $13,273.

### Owner Receives on Second Mortgage

| | |
|---|---|
| Total monthly payments | $ 3,600 |
| Balloon payment | 9,673 |
| Owner receives on second mortgage | $13,273 |

When we pointed out to the owner that he would effectively receive more than $53,000, we had his attention.

### Total Owner Receives

| | |
|---|---|
| Cash down payment | $40,000 |
| second mortgage | 13,273 |
| Total owner receives | $53,273 |

## *Risk*

The owner liked the numbers, but wanted to know what his risk would be extending us a second mortgage. When such questions arise, you shift into the education business. We told him we could default. He might have to foreclose on his second mortgage. He wanted to know how that would affect his equity.

We gave the owner the following scenario. Say we or a buyer we sold the property to defaults on his second mortgage and the first mortgage. The owner forecloses on his second mortgage. He winds up getting the property back subject to the remaining balance on the first mortgage.

The property is now worth $210,000. The first mortgage balance is $148,000. The owner has received $1,200 in monthly payments on the second mortgage. His foreclosure expenses including bringing the first mortgage current are $3,500. He has received the $40,000 cash down payment. How would he make out?

### Owner Forecloses on Second Mortgage

| | |
|---|---:|
| Property value | $210,000 |
| First mortgage balance | −148,000 |
| Owner equity position | $ 62,000 |
| Received down payment | 40,000 |
| Payments received on second mortgage | + 1,200 |
| Total gain | $103,200 |
| Foreclosure expenses | −3,500 |
| Owner's net gain | $ 99,700 |

We told him that not to be mean-spirited, but he could almost be forgiven for hoping we or a buyer we sold the property to defaults on the second mortgage! The owner would keep the $40,000 down payment plus the 12 months of payments and have an increased equity position when he regains ownership of the property after the foreclosure. Risk? What risk?

We told him the only risk is for him to reject our offer. Three or four months could go by before he gets another offer. Then, when that offer comes in for $190,000, he would jump on it. Besides losing $10,000 in equity, he would be out another $4,500 in mortgage payments, property taxes, and insurance premiums, making his net gain only $36,000. Needless to say after this presentation he accepted our offer.

**Owner Rejects Our Offer**

| | |
|---|---|
| New purchase price | $190,000 |
| Additional payments | 4,500 |
| First mortgage | −149,500 |
| Owner's net gain | $ 36,000 |

### Shoe on the Other Foot

Put yourself in the position of having made a property deal like we just did in the above example. Now you are the owner. Would you extend owner financing to make a deal to a new buyer? We hope your answer is yes.

The no-brainer aspect of extending owner financing for part of your equity should now be apparent. By being a flexible seller, you have greatly increased the number of potential buyers for your property. Those inflexible sellers who want all their equity in cash will give you the competitive edge in getting your property sold.

## Nothing Down

Let's take a look and see what happens if you sell your property and take all of your equity in mortgage notes. Why would you do this? Perhaps you may not need your equity in cash. Maybe you would like to have a monthly income.

How about you want a better return than putting your cash equity proceeds in the bank? You want the safety of an investment that is secured by real estate.

You are unwilling to take the risk of putting your money in the stock market.

Using the numbers we have already become familiar with, let's see what happens if you have a buyer who will pay $200,000 for your property, can afford to make the monthly payments on your $150,000 first mortgage, but has no money for a down payment. Should you automatically reject their offer? No! Let's look at the numbers.

Let's say you carry back the second mortgage for $50,000 at 7 percent annual interest, with monthly payments of $500, all due in 36 months. You would receive $18,000 in monthly payments. You would receive $41,681 as a balloon or final payment. Your total received would be $59,681.

### Total Received on Second Mortgage

| | |
|---|---|
| Monthly payments | $18,000 |
| Balloon payment | 41,681 |
| Total received on second mortgage | $59,681 |

Now you receive almost $210,000 for your property. Where else are you going to get a 7 percent return on an investment that is secured by real estate?

### Received for Property

| | |
|---|---|
| Assumed first mortgage | $150,000 |
| Total received on second mortgage | 59,681 |
| Received for property | $209,681 |

## Buyer Defaults

To be fair, let's see what happens if the buyer defaults on your second mortgage after 12 months. The buyer also defaults on the first mortgage. You foreclose on your second mortgage. You get the property back subject to the existing loan balance on the first mortgage.

The property is now worth $210,000. The first mortgage balance is now $148,000. You have received $6,000 in monthly payments. Your foreclosure expenses including bringing the first mortgage current are $3,500. How does this turn out for you?

### Owner Forecloses on Second Mortgage

| | |
|---|---|
| Property value | $210,000 |
| first mortgage balance | −148,000 |
| Owner equity position | $ 62,000 |
| Payments received on second mortgage | + 6,000 |
| Total gain | $ 68,000 |
| Foreclosure expenses | − 3,500 |
| Owner's net gain | $ 64,500 |

## Split the Notes

What if you are willing to take all of your equity in mortgage notes but want to have the possibility of converting some of that equity to cash before the balloon payments are due? One way you can do this is to split the mortgage notes. Instead of carrying a $50,000 second mortgage on the $200,000 home as in the previous example, what if you carried a $10,000 second mortgage and a $40,000 third mortgage?

Both the second and third mortgages would have a 7 percent annual interest rate and would be due in 36 months. The second mortgage would have $100 monthly payments. The third mortgage would have $400 monthly payments. So far, this would have the same net result as the $50,000 second mortgage; same interest rate, same due date, same total monthly payment.

Twelve months go by, and you need to get your hands on some quick cash. You will be able to sell the $10,000 second mortgage, which has a remaining balance of $9,484, for somewhere between $8,000 and $9,000.

Sell $10,000 second mortgage
Remaining balance $9,484

A real estate investor who purchases mortgage notes will gladly make you an offer on your second mortgage, which has been seasoned with 12 months of on-time payments. You get your quick cash for a minimal discount ($400 to $1,400) and the real estate investor has an 18 percent to 31 percent yield on his or her investment. (See our book, *The New Path to Real Estate Wealth: Earning Without Owning*, John Wiley & Sons, 2003, for information on this highly profitable area of real estate investing.)

If you were going to sell your $50,000 second mortgage, you might not be able to find a buyer because the combination of the first and second mortgages would create a loan-to-value ratio that would be too high. The balance on the $150,000 first mortgage would be $148,000. The balance on the $50,000 second mortgage would be $47,400. This would be a total loan balance of $195,400.

**Total Loan Balance**

| | |
|---|---|
| Balance on first mortgage | $148,000 |
| Balance on second mortgage | 47,400 |
| Total loan balance | $195,400 |

The property is now worth $210,000. This would be a loan-to-value ratio of 93 percent!

**Loan-to-Value Ratio**

$$\frac{\$195,400}{\$210,000} = 93\%$$

There is not enough equity beyond the financing to protect a real estate investor buying the second mortgage. The buyer of the second mortgage would want no more than an 80 percent investment-to-value-ratio.

The investment-to-value ratio is the combination of the remaining balance on the first mortgage and the amount of cash they are investing in buying your second mortgage. This would mean that the total of the balance on the first mortgage plus the cash invested in the second mortgage could be no more than $168,000.

### Investment-to-Value Ratio

$$\frac{\$168,000}{\$210,000} = 80\%$$

Since the remaining balance on the first mortgage is $148,000, at most you would receive $20,000 cash for your $47,400 equity in your second mortgage.

### Cash for Your Second Mortgage

| | |
|---|---:|
| Total investment-to-value ratio | $168,000 |
| Remaining balance on first mortgage | −148,000 |
| Cash for your second mortgage | $ 20,000 |

## Our Profit from Chapter 7

We told you in Chapter 7 that we would show you our profit on the deal here in Chapter 9. So how did we make out on this deal? Just to remind you, we had an instant equity position of $71,000 after making our short-sale deal. Within two weeks, we sold this property for $510,000.

### Our Equity

| | |
|---|---:|
| Property value | $510,000 |
| Negotiated lender payoff | −439,000 |
| Our equity | $ 71,000 |

We owned this property free and clear because we had paid cash to the lender doing the short-sale. We were in the perfect position to be the banker as the seller.

## Our Deal

We sold the property for $510,000. We received $110,000 in cash. We agreed to be the banker for the buyer and extend credit to him in the form of carrying a first mortgage. We carried a $400,000 mortgage note secured by a first mortgage.

### Being the Banker

| | |
|---|---:|
| First mortgage | $400,000 |
| Buyer's down payment | +110,000 |
| Sales price | $510,000 |

We got back $110,000 of our cash invested of $439,000 in the short-sale. This was a return of 25 percent.

$$\$110,000/\$439,000 = 25\%$$

We had converted the remaining $329,000 of our cash into a $400,000 first mortgage. Basically we had turned our $329,000 in cash into a $400,000 mortgage note that was producing cash flow. Why were we willing to do this? If we put our cash into a certificate of deposit we might get 3 percent annual interest. By being the banker we earned 7 percent on our mortgage note.

## Rule of 72

This is a good place to teach you the Rule of 72. The Rule of 72 states that whatever annual rate of return you receive on your investment, real estate or otherwise, your investment will double in the number of years you get as the answer to dividing 72 by the rate of return of the investment.

The Rule of 72 assumes you leave the investment return with the investment each year so you are compounding your investment return. We will assume your investment is in a tax-free or tax deferred vehicle.

Let's see how this works when you leave the money in the bank. If you receive 3 percent annual interest on $329,000 worth of certificates of deposit, then according to the Rule of 72 your $329,000 will become $658,000 in 24 years (72 divided by 3 percent is 24).

As a real estate banker who receives 7 percent annual interest on $400,000 worth of real estate loans, then according to the Rule of 72 our $400,000 will become $800,000 in 10 years (72 divided by 7 percent is 10 years).

| Certificates of Deposit | Real Estate Loans |
| --- | --- |
| $329,000 @ 3% | $400,000 @ 7% |
| 72/3 = 24 years | 72/7 = 10 years |
| Doubles to $658,000 | Doubles to $800,000 |

What is truly amazing about these numbers shows up if we look at them over the course of a 30-year real estate loan. Our $329,000 in CDs will double once to $658,000 in 24 years. Over the next six years (from 24 years to 30 years) our $658,000 will become $822,500. That's pretty good, right?

What do you think will happen to our $400,000 in mortgage loans? Our $400,000 in mortgage loans will double to $800,000 after 10 years, as we have already noted. The $800,000 will double to $1,600,000 in another 10 years (20 years total). The $1,600,000 will double to $3,200,000 in another 10 years (30 years total).

| Certificates of Deposit | Real Estate Loans |
| --- | --- |
| $329,000 @ 3% | $400,000 @ 7% |
| In 30 years | In 30 years |
| becomes | becomes |
| $822,500 | $3,200,000 |

Now you know why real estate lenders want to be in the real estate lending business. They make so much money on the interest rate spread. Real estate lenders do not want to be in the real estate owning business. This is a key factor in why real estate lenders will agree to make short-sale foreclosure deals.

In the next chapter we will show you how to Win Going In. This means you build a profit into the deal on the buying side before you pull the trigger on the deal. If you do not win going in the likelihood of making a profit on a deal is slim to none.

# Win Going In

We are going to introduce you to our real estate investment axiom: *Win going in.* This means you build a profit into the deal on the buying side before you pull the trigger on the deal. Our corollary axiom is *Buy the property first, then get a buyer.* Using these two axioms you are setting yourself up to be a successful investor.

By following these axioms it makes it easier for you to write offers. You do not have to fear what you are going to do if your offer is accepted! Writing an offer is the way to tie up a property. When you tie up a property you control a property.

## Tying Up a Property

When we traveled the United States teaching real estate investors Robert Allen's Nothing Down seminars, we blew students away with *buy the property first, then get the financing.* As we developed Howell Carey International University educational programs and traveled the world teaching them, you can imagine, since in short-sales you need cash to play, the shock when we said, "buy the property first, then get a buyer." In city after city, people told us we could not handle real estate investments this way. We told them to try it our way and report back to us what happened.

Sure enough, from Seattle to Orlando, from Los Angeles to Baltimore, from Chicago to Dallas, and then further—wherever we were—our students found that they could indeed not only buy the property first, then get the financing but they could also buy the property first, then get a buyer.

## Retail Buyer Mind-Set

Most, if not all, retail buyers (homebuyers or end users) have this mindset: How much money do I have to put down and how much of a monthly payment can I afford? With this mind-set, they go to a lender and hope to get prequalified for a real estate loan.

What the real estate lender says determines how much of a house the homebuyer thinks he or she can afford. Of course, being prequalified means nothing once you actually apply for a loan. You can be prequalified for a $200,000 loan and actually wind up receiving only a $175,000 loan at closing.

You are a real estate investor and not a homebuyer. You are a wholesale buyer of real estate. You are going to do things differently. Everyone, except us, will tell you to get your financing first, and then buy the property. We say tie up the property first, and then get the financing and/or buyer later according to your investment strategy. Let's take a look at a few deals.

## Buy the Property First, then Get the Financing or Buyer

### Example 1

We found a four-bedroom, two-bathroom, single-family home. The property was abandoned and headed to foreclosure. The retail value of the property was $159,000. The abandoned property owner had an assumable VA loan with a remaining balance of $129,000. He was $3,000 behind in his payments. He owed a total of $132,000 on his mortgage. His equity position was $27,000.

### Owner's Equity Position

| | |
|---|---|
| Retail value | $159,000 |
| Mortgage amount | −132,000 |
| Owner's equity position | $ 27,000 |

We called the number on the real estate sign and the agent asked us what we were prequalified for. This was our response and will be yours. We told the agent that we were real estate investors. If the property met our parameters, we had the financial resources, along with our money partners, to buy the property.

We set up an appointment with the agent and the abandoned property owner. We met with the agent and property owner to discuss what options were available. At the end of our meeting presentation, the property owners said they would like to sell us their property.

**Our Offer**   We offered them no money down and agreed to take over payments on the loan and make up the $3,000 in back payments. They accepted our offer. They agreed to pay their agent the real estate commission.

We did not have to qualify for a new loan. We did not have to qualify to take over the existing VA loan. We did not have to come up with a down payment. We made an offer that worked for us.

We let the abandoned property owner decide whether to accept our offer. We (and you) might not have accepted our offer. Why they accepted our offer was their business.

**Then Get a Buyer**   We now had a property available to flip. Only by making an offer can you start the process of flipping a property. We flipped the property for $139,000 within two weeks to a retail buyer who was going to live in the property.

The buyer was a veteran. He was going to use his VA eligibility to assume the loan. The buyer was very happy to get a good deal. The abandoned property owner was happy because he was out from under the foreclosure with no deficiency judgment hanging over his head. We were happy because we had made $7,000.

### Our Profit

| | |
|---|---|
| Sales price | $139,000 |
| Purchase price | 129,000 |
| Back payments | 3,000 |
| Our profit | $ 7,000 |

*Example 2*

We found a three-bedroom, two-bathroom, single-family home with a pool. The property was in foreclosure. The lender had sent the first formal notice of default letter. The owners were in a panic. They were thinking they were going to lose everything.

The retail value of the property was $210,000. The first mortgage on the property had a remaining balance of $155,000. The owners were $9,000 behind in their payments. Their equity position was $46,000.

### Owner's Equity Position

| | |
|---|---:|
| Retail value | $210,000 |
| Mortgage amount | 155,000 |
| Back payments | 9,000 |
| Owner's equity position | $ 46,000 |

**Our Offer**   We offered the owners $10,000 for their equity in the form of a promissory note secured by a second trust deed on the property. The promissory note was a straight note for three years. This means there were no payments until the final balloon payment of principal and interest at the end of the three years.

We also agreed to pay the $9,000 in back payments and reinstate the loan. The total cash out of our pocket was $9,000. Remember the $10,000 we offered the owners for their equity was a promissory note and not cash. We were not worried about this promissory note because we were going to flip the property.

**Then Get a Buyer**   We flipped the property for $185,000. The buyer was a real estate investor who was planning on renting the property. He assumed the first mortgage of $155,000 from the lender and our second mortgage of $10,000 to the owners.

We were now off the hook for paying the owners. Because the $10,000 second mortgage had no payments, the real estate investor would have a positive cash flow.

How did we make out on this deal? We invested $9,000 cash and received our money back plus an $11,000 profit. The owners avoided foreclosure and had $10,000 plus interest coming their way three years down the road. The investor was happy because he got a good deal.

### Our Profit

| | |
|---|---|
| Sales price | $185,000 |
| First mortgage | 155,000 |
| Second mortgage | 10,000 |
| Back payments | 9,000 |
| Our profit | $ 11,000 |

Some of you are thinking, "Why didn't you guys hold onto the property like the investor you flipped the property to, rent it out, or sell it being the bank and have a positive cash flow?" That is good thinking if you are using the long-term wealth building strategy. We had a quick cash strategy at the time, so becoming landlords or being the bank was not on our agenda for that deal.

## Example 3

We tied up a three-bedroom, three-bathroom, single-family home with a pool. The owners were underwater. We negotiated a deal with the owners and had our short-sale offer accepted by the lender. We then spent $8,000 fixing up the property.

We are presenting this example here as a way of coaching you on what not to do. This was not one of our finest hours. We were still in the more traditional mind-set of trying to make everyone in the deal happy. By the time this deal blew up, no one was happy.

**Then Get a Buyer**   We found retail buyers who said they were in love with the house. To make the deal work, we agreed to repaint the inside of the house, which we had just painted, using the colors the buyers wanted.

We also agreed to run a natural gas line to the utility room so the buyers could use their gas dryer. Finally, we had a tree removed from the pool area because the buyers were concerned that the roots were going to crack the bottom of the pool.

Can you guess what happened? The buyers came down with a disease so many retail buyers get during the course of a real estate transaction. Some buyers get a mild case of the disease. Some buyers get a severe case of the disease. Unfortunately for us, these particular buyers came down with a terminal case of the disease.

**Buyer's Remorse**   What is this dreaded disease? Buyer's Remorse! Every buyer experiences the onset of the disease once their offer is accepted by the seller. Even as a real estate investor, you will experience buyer's remorse. There is no known antidote or medication. The disease just has to run its course.

The symptoms of Buyer's Remorse usually strike at night, when a buyer is about to go to sleep. Sometimes the symptoms strike after the buyer has fallen asleep and then awakens as if from a nightmare.

The buyers start having doubts about the purchase. Are they doing the right thing? Should they look at more properties? Did they offer too much? Can they really afford the monthly payments? Is the house big enough? Is the house too big?

They start to sweat. They get out of bed and get a drink of water. They go back to bed, but they can't fall asleep. The questions begin swirling again in their heads. What if they don't qualify for a loan? What if they *do* qualify for a loan? Who is going to take care of the pool? What if the pool does leak?

In our case, three weeks after we had accepted the buyers' offer, and three days after we had finished repainting, installing the gas line, and removing the tree, the buyers backed out. Their case of remorse became terminal for them and for us. Our deal was dead.

Bottom line: Provide allowances for the work to be done *after* closing, if you must, to make the deal work, but don't spend your time or money on it before closing. Oh yes, and our profit on this deal? Don't ask. You got the point, right?

## Example 4

The other problem with retail buyers is they usually do not pay cash for their real estate purchases. They have to qualify for and obtain a loan from a real estate lender. This means you will have to wait longer to get your money. Forty-five days is a fairly standard closing period from the time an offer is accepted to get a loan processed and funded.

In the case of a government-insured loan or a government-guaranteed loan such as an FHA loan or a VA loan, it may take anywhere from 45 to 75 days to fund the loan and close the escrow.

**Our Offer**   We tied up a three-bedroom, one-and-a-half-bathroom condo that was in preforeclosure. We bought it for nothing down and took over the owners' existing loan of $77,000.

**Then Get a Buyer**    We flipped the condo to a retail buyer who made an FHA offer to us for $89,000. This looked like a sure moneymaker for us because we only had $2,000 into the property for back payments on the loan.

### Our Potential Profit

| | |
|---|---:|
| Sales price | $89,000 |
| Purchase price | 77,000 |
| Back payments | −2,000 |
| Our profit potential | $10,000 |

The escrow was to close in 45 days or fewer. When it finally closed after 79 days, we had several unexpected surprises. The first surprise was that the deal actually closed. That was a nice surprise. The other surprises were not so nice.

We had almost three months of interest due on the old loan being paid off. We had almost three months of property taxes to pay. And we had almost three months of homeowner's association dues to pay as well. These costs were really starting to add up.

The *coup de grace* was the four discount points we had to pay on the $84,000 FHA government-insured loan. Each discount point was 1 percent of the loan amount. This amounted to $840! We had no idea this was going to be so expensive. Needless to say, we were not happy with what happened to our $10,000 potential profit.

### Actual Profit
### (Potential Profit $10,000)

| | |
|---|---:|
| Loan interest | $1,540 |
| Property taxes | 750 |
| Homeowner's dues | 353 |
| FHA discount points | 3,360 |
| Actual profit | $3,997 |

While we were upset because the potential profit had been eaten up we were glad we still had something to show for the time we had invested in the deal. Now let's talk about wholesale buyers.

# Wholesale Buyers

We prefer to flip, and recommend that you flip, properties to wholesale buyers. Wholesale buyers do not get buyer's remorse. (Well, maybe a very mild case.) We know some of you are thinking, "Wait a minute. How can you make any money flipping real estate to wholesale buyers? Don't wholesale buyers want to pay a wholesale price?"

We do flip our property deals at a wholesale price to wholesale buyers! We are not greedy about it. We prefer to do many smaller deals and make a quick profit rather than one or two big deals that are very time-consuming and entail more risk.

We have come to appreciate that being successful real estate investors is strictly a numbers game. Although we prefer to flip our properties to other investors for all the reasons we just talked about, we are still smart people.

Our marketplace includes retail and wholesale buyers. The more buyers you have in your potential pool, the more likely you will be able to flip your property deals successfully.

## Negotiating with the Owner's Lender

Next, we are going to talk about negotiating with the property owner's lender before the foreclosure sale. This may be before or after you have put an agreement together with the property owner to buy his equity or his property.

### *Negotiating before You Put the Agreement Together*

We suggest you consider negotiating with the lender before you have put any agreement together with the property owner. That way you will know how the lender is going to behave. This will eliminate any nasty surprises from the lender down the road. You will need the property owners' permission to speak with their lender. Of course, talking to the lender does not guarantee that you and the sellers will then see eye to eye, but it is, nevertheless, something to seriously consider.

While we recommend that you dispose of properties quickly, especially foreclosures, you may have to hold on to a property longer than you planned. One of the most important areas to negotiate is how the lender is going to respond if you buy the owner's equity and want to take over the existing loan. Most real estate loans have a due-on-sale clause and/or a prepayment penalty.

### *Lender Plays Hardball*

If the lender wants to play hardball, it can begin foreclosure proceedings against you if you don't agree with what it wants to do with the loan vis-à-vis interest rates, assumption fees, payment amounts, or prepayment penalties. We are going to give you an overview of the due-on-sale clause. We will also show you the difference between an assumable loan and a subject-to loan. Also, there may be a prepayment penalty to be considered. Remember Ray Vargas from Chapter 1 and his prepayment penalty nightmare? Let's start with the due-on-sale clause.

**Due-on-Sale Clause**    A due-on-sale clause is a type of acceleration clause in a promissory note, mortgage note, trust deed, or mortgage contract that gives a lender the right to demand all sums owed to be paid immediately if the owner transfers title to the property.

In the United States the legality of the due-on-sale clause was argued all the way to the Supreme Court in the 1980s. To unify all the states under one legal interpretation, Congress passed the Garn-St. Germain lending bill in 1986. Unfortunately the due-on-sale clause is legal. It can be enforced by the lenders.

**Assumable Loan**    An assumable loan is an existing promissory note or mortgage note secured by a trust deed or mortgage contract, respectively, that is kept at the same interest rate and terms stipulated when the original borrower financed the property.

When you assume a loan you become primarily liable for the payments and any deficiency judgment arising from a loan default. The borrower/owner becomes secondarily liable for the payments and any deficiency judgment.

Remember, a deficiency judgment is a court decision making an individual personally liable for the payoff of a remaining amount due because less than the full amount was obtained by foreclosure on the property.

Lenders typically charge an assumption fee for you to assume a loan. They also want you to qualify for the loan, as if you were originating a new loan rather than assuming an existing loan.

**Subject-To Loan**    A subject-to loan is an existing loan for which the buyer agrees to take over responsibility for payments under the same terms and conditions as existed when the original borrower financed the property. However, the original borrower remains primarily responsible for any deficiency judgment in the event of a loan default.

The name subject-to loan comes from the fact that the buyer takes over the existing loan subject-to the same terms and conditions. The interest rate is the same. The monthly payments are the same. Everything about the loan stays the same. There is no lender approval required for you to take over a loan subject-to as there is when you assume a loan.

We say it this way. When you assume a loan you are entering into a formal agreement with the lender. When you take over a loan subject-to there is no formal agreement with the lender. Subject-to loans do not have a due-on-sale clause in their paperwork.

Therefore, the lender cannot threaten you with calling the loan due-on-sale when you have made a deal with the owner to transfer title. In the United States pre-1988 VA guaranteed loans and pre-1986 FHA insured loans are subject-to loans. Also, many privately held owner financing loans may be subject-to loans.

## Prepayment Penalty

A prepayment penalty is a fine imposed on a borrower by a lender for early payoff of a loan or any early payoff of a substantial part of the loan. To find out if there is a prepayment penalty on a loan, check the loan documents. Most prepayment penalties lapse once the loan is on the books for five years.

The amount of the prepayment penalty is usually stated as a certain number of months of interest payments in addition to the amount remaining on the loan as of the payoff date. Prepayment penalties can be six months of interest or more. This can be quite a substantial amount.

What is the prepayment penalty on a loan if the remaining loan balance is $200,000, the annual interest rate is 7 percent, and the prepayment penalty is 6 months interest?

### Prepayment Penalty

| | |
|---|---|
| Loan balance | $200,000 |
| Interest rate | × 7% |
| Annual interest | $ 14,000 |
| 6 months interest | $ 7,000 |

A lender cannot legally enforce receiving a prepayment penalty as a result of a foreclosure sale. The problem for you as a real estate investor is that the prohibition on the lender receiving a prepayment penalty as a result of a foreclosure sale is lifted if you buy the owner's equity in preforeclosure.

**Whipsaw Effect**   A lender can have an owner/borrower, or in this case, you, an investor caught between the due-on-sale clause and the prepayment penalty. You are attempting to help the owners out of a foreclosure situation by buying their equity. You may encounter what we call the whipsaw effect with the lender.

If you try to take over the owner's existing loan subject-to and it is not a subject-to loan, the lender can call the loan due and payable using the due-on-sale clause. If you tell the lender you are going to pay off the loan, and the loan is fewer than five years old and stipulates a prepayment penalty, you may get stuck paying the prepayment penalty. We move on now to negotiating with the lender after you have put an agreement together with the owner.

## Negotiating after You Put the Agreement Together

You may prefer negotiating with the lender after you have put an agreement together with the owner. As we stated earlier, there is no guarantee that you will be able to come to an agreement with the seller after you talk to the lender. Some investors find it a waste of time to negotiate with the lender before they have put a written agreement together with the owner. After they have gotten their ducks lined up with the lender, they then find they cannot reach an agreement to buy the owner's equity or property.

## Talking to the Lender

The earlier in the foreclosure process the lender is contacted, the better it is for the borrower. Sometimes a borrower will call the lender and say, "We haven't missed a payment yet, but we are afraid we are about to." Lenders agree that they want to know about a borrower's financial distress well ahead of the borrower missing that first loan payment.

As far as the lender is concerned, this is the perfect time for the owner in distress to call them. A spokeswoman for Fannie Mae puts it this way: "Don't hide from your lender. If you contact your loan servicer, most of the time you will stay in your home."

After you receive an owner's permission to talk to his lender, we suggest the following approach. Call the lender and identify yourself as a real estate investor who is working with the owner. Find out from the lender exactly where the owner is in the foreclosure process.

It has been our experience that half the time some type of loan workout plan is put together between the lender and the owner. The other half of the time when a loan workout plan is not put together is when you have your opportunity to make money.

You want to know three things from the lender. How much time will you have to flip the property? How much money will it cost to delay the foreclosure sale? Will the lender consider a short-sale if the property owner is underwater?

This chapter has been about how to win going into a deal. You have to buy for the right price and with the right terms. In the next chapter we will discuss how to sell for the right terms and for the right price. We call this No Doubt Getting Out.

# CHAPTER 11

# No Doubt Getting Out

In this chapter we discuss how to sell for the right terms and for the right price. We call this No Doubt Getting Out. If you are using the quick cash strategy with a property, you would be flipping the property.

## When to Flip

It has been our experience as real estate investors that there is no "right" time to flip real estate. What we want to teach you in this chapter is the answer to the question: "When are the best times to flip real estate?" In other words, how do you determine when to flip?

That is easy. Flip the property before you make an offer on it. Flip the property after you have made an offer on it. Flip the property before you close escrow. Flip the property after you close escrow. In other words, flip property any time. Any time you can make money, that is.

What if you flip a property too soon? Is this bad? Should you have waited for the second or third real estate investor to come along? Our experience tells us that if you have a deal, take it. The old adage "a bird in the hand is worth two in the bush," must have been coined by a real estate investor.

## Flipping before You Write the Offer

Can you flip property before you write the offer? Sure, why not? There is no rule or law that says you have to write an offer first before you flip a property. However, there is one caveat.

### Caveat

The one caveat we will give you about flipping property before you have had your written offer accepted by the seller is this. You must have something in writing with the potential buyer to protect yourself before you give that individual any information about the property or the seller.

How do you protect yourself as a real estate investor in a real estate transaction where an offer has not been presented to, let alone accepted by, the seller? What is to prevent a potential buyer of your flipped property from going directly to the seller after you tell the buyer about the property and cutting you out?

### Nondisclosure and Noncircumvention Agreement

It is important to protect yourself in any real estate transaction. That is why we stressed CoCa CoLa (Consent, Capacity, Consideration, Lawful) as part of any real estate contract. We also said that in order for a real estate contract to be valid, it must be in writing.

This is where a nondisclosure and noncircumvention agreement comes into play. It becomes the agreement before the real estate contract. We are going to give you an example of a simple nondisclosure, noncircumvention agreement we use to give us protection with potential buyers of a property that we have not yet tied up with a real estate purchase contract.

## Nondisclosure and Noncircumvention Agreement

*This is intended to be a legally binding agreement.*

1.    This is to confirm that each of the named INTRODUCED SIGNATORIES will not make any contact with, deal with, or

otherwise get involved in any real estate transaction with the named seller(s) without express written permission of the INTRODUCING SIGNATORIES.

Named Seller(s): _____

2. By signature below and execution of this Agreement, each of the named SIGNATORIES confirm that any association they would benefit from financially is bound by this Agreement.

3. The INTRODUCED SIGNATORIES hereby agree to keep completely confidential the names of any sellers introduced by the INTRODUCING SIGNATORIES. It is understood this Agreement is a reciprocal one between the parties concerning their privileged information and contacts.

4. Essentially the spirit behind this Agreement is one of MUTUAL TRUST AND CONFIDENCE, and of the reliance of each party to do what is fair and equitable for all parties concerned.

5. This Agreement is signed and agreed to on this __ day of 20___ by the below signed individuals.

Introducing Signatories      Introduced Signatories

Why would we bother to show a potential buyer a property we have not gotten an accepted offer on? Why don't we just wait till we get our offer accepted so we don't need a nondisclosure and noncircumvent agreement?

### Network of Real Estate Investors

We have a network of real estate investors who specialize in fixer-up property.

We have them look at property that we have found to get an estimate on what it will cost to make the property saleable.

They also give us a price they would be willing to pay for the property. We then have a range of prices and buyers who we can flip the property to. This helps us to know how to negotiate with the seller.

### Example

We found a property that was a bomb. Not bomb as in *the* bomb. Bomb as in the property needed to be blown up. The property had been vacant for a year. We knew we needed to strip everything back to the studs.

We thought we might have to use torching methods to kill the rats, mice, roaches, fleas, molds, and bacteria that called this place home.

**The Flea Dance**    When we were about to get back in our vehicle after looking at the inside of this property for the first time, Chantal screamed, "Don't get in!" We looked down at our clothing. We were covered in fleas! We were fresh meat that had just walked in the door. We spent the next 30 minutes doing the flea dance.

First Bill would brush Chantal off, and then Chantal would brush Bill off. Then we would have to move 20 feet away so the fleas we had just brushed off did not jump back on. We laughed later in the day when we realized how funny we must have looked to anyone watching from afar and not knowing we had become a feast for fleas!

**Help**    While our Property Potential Vision was going crazy, we were still hesitant to make an offer without some help. Because our construction and remodeling expertise is not as extensive as this property would require, we wanted to show the property to real estate investors with more construction and remodeling expertise. We were looking for a second and a third opinion.

We approached three real estate investors who we knew were in the fix-up business. We had each of them sign the nondisclosure and noncircumvention agreement. Then we showed the three investors the property at three different times. By the way, on these subsequent visits we all wore bib overalls or jumpsuits over our clothing.

One investor said the property could be fixed for $25,000. The second investor said the property could be fixed for $35,000. The third investor said he wouldn't touch the property with a 10-foot pole!

**Our Offer**    With the information from our investors, we wrote an offer on the property for the land value. Without our investors' help we would have overpaid for the property. We told the seller that the building was basically worthless. We would have to completely gut the building and start over. The owner was asking $62,000. We offered the owner $39,000 cash. We bought the property for $39,000.

### Our Offer

| | |
|---|---|
| Asking price | $62,000 |
| Our offer | $39,000 |
| Purchase price | $39,000 |

Now we needed to flip the property. Which one of the three real estate investors do you think we flipped the property to? Did we flip the property to the first real estate investor who gave us a $25,000 fix-up estimate? Did we flip the property to the second real estate investor who gave us a $35,000 fix-up estimate? Or, did we flip the property to the third investor who was the one who wouldn't touch the property with a 10-foot pole?

**Our Flip**   We flipped the property to the real estate investor who wouldn't touch the property with a 10-foot pole! We told him about the $25,000 and $35,000 estimates from the other two investors, and he decided he might just be able to make some money on the deal. We flipped it to him for $52,000.

**Our Flip**

| | |
|---|---|
| Sales price | $52,000 |
| Purchase price | 39,000 |
| Profit | $13,000 |

## Flipping after You Write the Offer

We have found that we flip the majority of our properties after we write the offer and have it accepted by the seller. This gives us more control of the entire situation. Once we have our offer accepted the seller knows we are a serious buyer. The seller also feels more comfortable giving us access to the property the multiple times we may need to take potential buyers through the property.

### *Modus Operandi*

We want you to understand our modus operandi here. Investors have been flipping real estate for hundreds of years. We are following in that great tradition with several important improvements. Most real estate investors flip property after they take title to the property, in other words, after they have closed escrow. We are taking you into new territory.

This new territory includes flipping property before you write an offer. It also includes flipping property after writing an offer, and flipping property before you close escrow.

## Flipping without Owning

You may be thinking of a question here. You may have grasped the fact that flipping real estate is easy if you are flipping property you own. If you own the property you have the title to the property in the form of a grant deed or a warranty deed depending upon what ownership deed is used in your area.

After you make a deal with the new buyer and flip them your property you give them ownership of the property by giving them a new grant deed or warranty deed. You could even use a quit claim deed. If you already own the property, it is easy for you to sell or flip your ownership interest in the property to a new buyer.

Your question is: How do you flip real estate you don't own? That is a very good question! It turns out that if you do it this way, you are not in the real estate investment business at all. That would imply that you invest in real estate. It would imply that you own real estate. Flipping real estate you don't own more accurately puts you in the real estate wholesale deal business!

### *Real Estate Wholesale Deal Business*

We are in the real estate wholesale deal business! We negotiate a great deal with an owner of a property. In other words, we tie the property up. We find a new buyer. This could be a retail or a wholesale buyer. Then we flip the deal to the new buyer.

We don't flip the property. The property just happens to come along with the deal. If the new buyer is a wholesale buyer, he is going to flip the property again to a retail buyer. We are interested in owning real estate for just as long as it takes to flip a deal. The real estate just happens to be the lawful subject of the deal.

### *Assigning*

When you read Chapter 15: Buy Low and Sell Lower, you will get the full picture of what we are talking about here. What you want to take away from this discussion now is that there is a way to flip real estate without owning it.

In fact, what you are assigning are real estate contracts. Once you can grasp this concept you are going to be like a real estate kid in a real estate candy store. Does anyone smell money?

## Flipping before You Close Escrow

We flip 95 percent to 98 percent of our deals before we close escrow. What is the difference between flipping after you write the offer and flipping before you close escrow? The difference between flipping after you write the offer and flipping before you close escrow depends on when you find a new buyer for your deal.

## Finding a New Buyer

If you find a new buyer after your write the offer and before you open an escrow, the new buyer will open escrow with the seller. If you find a new buyer after you open escrow and before you close escrow, the escrow between you and the seller will have to be amended to reflect the new buyer as the other party to the seller in the escrow. You will not be a party to the escrow any longer.

This difference will become more apparent as we go through other sections of this book. For now, suffice it to say that if you can flip a deal after writing your offer and before opening an escrow, you will save valuable time and make money more quickly.

If you have to wait to flip a deal till after you open escrow you may also incur some additional expenses. You may be responsible for paying for the preliminary title report. You may also be responsible for paying for part or all of the buyer's side of the escrow fees.

## Flipping after You Close Escrow

Most real estate investors flip properties after they close escrow. Most real estate investors are more comfortable closing escrow on a property and owning it first before they flip it. You have to find your own comfort zone between the real estate wholesale deal business and the real estate investing world.

What we want to expose you to ultimately are ways to make money in real estate without buying or owning property. Since this chapter is about when to flip property, we are including this traditional time of flipping property: after closing escrow.

Please do not misunderstand. Plenty of real estate investors have made plenty of money flipping real estate after the close of escrow. And we are not saying that owning real estate is a bad thing. We just sometimes prefer making money in real estate investing without buying or owning the property.

## Timeline for Flipping

This is probably a good place to make a timeline so you can easily visualize when the different periods to flip your deals occur. What we are saying is new here is anything to do with flipping your deal up to and including flipping your deal before you close escrow.

Up till the close of escrow you are flipping the deal and not the property. You don't own the property and hence can't flip the property till after escrow closes. After escrow closes you do own the property and you are flipping the property and not the deal. Flipping the property is the same old stuff.

### Timeline for Flipping Deals

| **Write Offer** | **Open Escrow** | **Close Escrow** | |
|---|---|---|---|
| Flip | Flip | Flip | Flip |
| Before | After | After | After |
| Writing | Writing | Opening | Closing |
| Offer | Offer | Escrow | Escrow |
| New | New | New | Old |

### *Deal Flip Summary*

You can flip your deal before writing an offer with the help of the nondisclosure and noncircumvention agreement. You and the new buyer sign the nondisclosure and noncircumvention agreement. You show the new buyer the property. You flip the new buyer the deal after the new buyer helps you determine a price to offer the seller.

You can flip your deal after writing your offer to a new buyer. You can do the flip either before you open an escrow or after you open an escrow. In either case you will make money on your flip. And you can flip the property after escrow closes.

Flipping is a two-step process. The first step is to tie up a property. This is otherwise known as making an offer. The second step is to find a buyer. This is known as making money on your deal. This is the purpose of flipping and is the quick cash strategy in action.

## Flipping Your Short-Sales

When you flip short-sales you use the same techniques as flipping non-short-sales, but with a few modifications. Buy the short-sale first, and then get a buyer is our short-sale axiom. Actually, buying the short-sale and finding a buyer to flip it to are simultaneous activities.

Up until 2005, we were able to flip our short-sales in a simultaneous closing. We would make a deal with the property owner in distress who had little or no equity in their property to do a short-sale. We would then present our short-sale offer to the lender. As the lender was accepting our short-sale deal we lined up potential retail buyers to flip the property to.

## New Lending Laws

This all changed in the United States with the new lending laws. Now you have to have two separate and distinct transactions in your short-sale investing. You have to go in and cash out the short-sale lender in order to get title to the property. Then you can turn around and immediately sell your short-sale property to a new buyer.

You can still flip your short-sale contract by assigning the contract to another short-sale buyer. Just be aware of this caveat: Many lenders are unreceptive to assigning any real estate contracts let alone a short-sale contract.

As with any real estate investing, the good deal is the most important requirement. Finding the money to fund your good deal is the easy part. We know money investors who will loan cash to us to fund our short-sale deals at 15 percent interest and 3 points. Given we need the money for 30 to 60 days, the actual cash cost for the financing is fairly minimal in comparison to the amount of money we recoup once we sell the property to a retail buyer.

### *Example*

Here is an example so you can see what we mean. We had a short-sale offer accepted for $150,000 cash. We wanted to commit only $100,000 of our cash. We borrowed $50,000 from an investor for 60 days at 15 percent annual interest.

**Borrowing Funds**

| | |
|---|---|
| Short-sale price | $150,000 |
| Our cash | −100,000 |
| Borrowed funds | $ 50,000 |

This cost us $1,250 and $1,500 in points for a total of $2,750.

**Interest and Points Cost**

| | |
|---|---|
| Interest | $1,250 |
| Points | +1,500 |
| Total | $2,750 |

We sold this property for $209,000. We made $56,250 after repaying the loan, the interest and the points.

**Profit**

| | |
|---|---|
| Sale price | $209,000 |
| Our cash | 100,000 |
| Loan | 50,000 |
| Interest & points | −2,750 |
| Profit | $ 56,250 |

We hope this last example will make some lightbulbs go on for some of you. Short-sale investing is only going to get more lucrative. By getting involved in this exciting real estate foreclosure arena now, you will be ensuring a bright financial future. We predict that because some of you will read this book and become short-sale foreclosure investors, the number of multimillionaires in the world will go up!

## Other Creative Agreements

Buyers and sellers often use agreements in addition to, in combination with, or instead of the purchase offer. For example, a property owner may lease his property to you before closing. You may lease the property to the property owner after closing. You may lease the property with an option to buy. The property owner may give you just an option to buy.

We have found that when we invest in real state in a crashing market we need to bring our entire real estate contract arsenal with us to the negotiating table. For the rest of this chapter we will present some of the other creative agreements we use in our real estate investing. Each one gives you another way to sell for the right terms and the right price.

## Lease

A *lease* is a contract by which one party (lessor) transfers possession and use of property for a limited, designated term at a specified price and under the stipulated conditions to another party (lessee).

You can buy blank lease forms at your local stationery store or in some states from your Board of Realtors. Books available at your local library or bookstore contain sample leases. Consult with your attorney or a real estate professional if you have questions concerning leasing.

Leasing a property rather than buying it can protect your investment capital. If you lease all or part of a property after you buy it then you can obtain income from a property that otherwise might be costing you money to hold on to.

The disadvantage to a lease is that the lessees (renters) may not pay the rent. They can be difficult to remove from the property if there is a problem.

Lessees may cause considerable damage before you can remove them from the property.

## Option

An option is a contract that gives potential buyers (optionees) the right to purchase a property before the specified future date for the amount and under the conditions listed in the contract. Also, buyers agree to pay an added amount (an option fee) if they do not use the option.

The seller does not receive money for the sale until the property is sold, usually near or at the end of the option period. Unless you negotiate otherwise, the property owner cannot legally raise the property's price during the term of the option.

Some investors recommend using an attorney to draw up the option agreement. We recommend this only if it will make you feel more comfortable or if it is part of a very complex property deal. We have found options a very useful tool when investing in property.

We will mention here that by using an option the price of the property can be determined by a mutually acceptable method between us and the property owner at the time we exercise the option. This has helped us stay out of some bad deals.

## Lease Purchase Agreements

If you lease a property during the period before escrow closes, use a lease in combination with the purchase contract or a consolidated form, such as an Interim Occupancy Agreement. This gives the property owner an income that can help his cash flow. This gives you an opportunity to discover things about the property that you may not like. It also may save you from doing a bad deal.

On the other hand, if you are leasing the property, you may have difficulty getting buyers to vacate the property if they refuse to go through with the sale.

Buyers who refuse to complete the sale might cause considerable damage before you can remove them.

## Sale Leaseback Agreement

If you rent or lease the property to the property owner after escrow closes, use a lease in combination with a purchase contract or a specific sale leaseback form, such as an Interim Occupancy Agreement. This may also work in combination with an equity share agreement between you and the property owner.

### Equity Share

The property owners may have moved out of the property fearing a foreclosure. By putting an equity share deal together with you, they may move back into the property. In return for you making up the back mortgage payments, you get a 50 percent ownership interest in the property.

## Lease Option

If you agree to lease your property with an option to buy, use a lease option or a combination of a lease, an option, and a purchase contract. This enables you to obtain income from a property that otherwise might be costing you money. If the buyers do not exercise the option, you get to keep the option fee.

Your buyers can decide to purchase your property at any time within the lease period. You do not receive money for the sale until the property is sold, usually near or at the end of the lease period. Unless you negotiate otherwise, you cannot legally increase the property price during the contract.

Remember, after the buyers live in the property, they may discover certain inconveniences or problems that they did not expect leading them to prefer living in the property without purchasing it.

### *Points to Consider*

If you decide to use a lease option, think about requesting approval for the lease option from an existing lender. The loan may contain a due-on-sale clause that could be triggered by a lease option. Include a provision for buyers to forfeit their security deposit if they decide not to purchase the property on a lease option. Add a clause that buyers make monthly lease payments to equal or exceed payments on the existing loan. You may want to insert a provision that you credit buyers with a portion of the monthly lease payment toward the purchase price.

## Reverse Lease Option (Sale Leaseback with Option to Purchase)

As a final creative solution we give you the reverse lease option. When we think of lease options, we think of leasing the property with an option to purchase it at some point in the future at some agreed upon price.

A sales twist on this technique is to purchase the property and lease it back to the owners. You also give them an option to purchase the property at some point in the future at some agreed upon price.

The agreed upon future price should include any cash you put into paying the delinquent mortgage payment and property taxes plus any negative cash flow (if applicable) and an acceptable return on your investment. As with the equity sharing arrangement, consult with your attorney for assistance in structuring the transaction.

## Purchase Option

A purchase option contract states that potential buyers have the right to purchase the property before the specified future date for the amount listed and under the conditions specified in the contract. Also, they agree to pay an option fee that is applied to the purchase price if they exercise the option. If they don't exercise the option, the option fee is forfeited.

If you agree to grant a purchase option, use a purchase option form or a combination option and purchase contract. You cannot increase the price for your property during the term of the contract. A price increase is illegal even if all other properties in the area increase substantially in value.

Our goal for this chapter has been to have you think creatively about structuring your deals. Creative finance may be the only way to put together a win-win deal. Your job is to educate owners when you are buying and buyers when you are selling on the creative financing that will be to both of your overall financial benefit.

In the next chapter we begin our discussion of auctioning. Auctioning may be the best way to sell your property in a crashing real estate market. Real estate lenders use foreclosure auctions to sell their REOs. If lenders are making money auctioning why can't we make money auctioning?

# CHAPTER 12

# Auctioning Your Property for Top Dollar

Every real estate transaction is actually an auction. Whether you list your property with a real estate broker or sell it yourself you are going to sell your property to the highest bidder. With either one of these traditional ways of selling your property you, the seller, are under tremendous emotional, financial, and time pressure.

## Traditional Selling

Let us briefly review how these traditional ways of selling real estate work (or don't work). The real estate broker or you advertise the property, hold open houses, and watch potential buyers dribble through over a period of weeks or months. You hope to get that one buyer who will make you a full price—or at least an acceptable—offer. The problem is that the buyers, and not you, are in control of the sales process.

## No or Low Offers

After two to three months of no or low offers you become frustrated and then tend to jump unwisely at the first or next offer even if it is too low. We will show you how to have a faster sale with a higher price by creating and using *buyer compression.*

Buyer compression brings multiple buyers into a veritable feeding frenzy where the emotional, financial, and time pressure is all on the buyers to bid. Instead of the buyers being in control of the sales process, you are now in control of selling your home!

## Auction Scenario

We want to give you a taste of auctioning your property for top dollar in the following auction scenario. You would like to sell your property for $200,000. You assemble potential buyers (bidders) and have your auctioneer open the bidding at $150,000. Within the first minute bidder number 6 bids $160,000, bidder number 4 bids $170,000, and bidder number 1 bids $175,000.

At this point you would be unhappy if the bidding stopped. So far, the bidders are all comfortable with the fact that if they could get your property for their bid they would have made a very good purchase. Now buyer compression comes into play.

## Buyer Compression

Bidder number 3 is the Greens. Their best friends, the Hoppers, have just moved into your neighborhood. The Greens want your property and will pay whatever price it takes to get it. Bidder number 6, Mr. and Mrs. Low; bidder number 4, Mr. and Mrs. Ball; and bidder number 1, Mr. and Mrs. Player; are investors looking for a good deal.

They have been influenced by infomercials on how to buy property at real estate foreclosure auctions. Unfortunately for them they do not understand that you and your property are not in foreclosure. Fortunately for you they have come to your auction and started the bidding. They will bid no higher.

Bidder number 5 is the Pitches, and they like your property. They want to buy it as their home and at a good price. The Pitches bid $190,000. This is called a shutout bid. The Pitches are hoping the sharp increase from the Player's bid of $175,000 will discourage anyone else from bidding. Bidder number 7 is the Craftys. They have been waiting for the shutout bid.

The Craftys bid $191,000. The Greens can't stand it any longer. They are surprised at how quickly the other bidders have bid up the price. The Greens bid $195,000. The Pitches decide to make one more bid. They bid $196,000. The Greens bid $199,000.

The Greens are getting excited! The auctioneer asks for more bids. None are forthcoming. The auctioneer says: "Going once" (for $199,000) . . . the Greens can hardly stand it! . . . "going twice" . . . they are about to get their dream home! . . . they can taste victory! Just before the auctioneer says "Gone! Sold to bidder number 3 for $199,000!" bidder number 13 bids $205,000!

## Hearts in Throats

The Greens' hearts are in their throats. The Greens think, "Who the hell is bidder number 13?" The Greens crane their swollen necks to glare at their rival and realize "Oh my God!" Bidder number 13 is the Hoppers' cousins, the Mantises!

As if their heads are under water, the Greens hear the auctioneer's muffled voice intone: "Going once (for $205,000) . . . going twice" . . . Mrs. Green elbows Mr. Green in the ribs . . . at the same time she tries to whisper but instead screams in his ear, "Bid!" Mr. Green blurts outs, "$209,000!" "Going once . . . going twice . . . gone! Sold to bidder number 3 for $209,000!"

## A Happy Ending

The Greens are ecstatic! They won! Thank God they repelled the preying of the Mantises! They will be moving into the same neighborhood as their friends, the Hoppers. There is also another very happy person at the conclusion of this three-minute auction—you!

You have just auctioned your property for top dollar! You just sold your property for $9,000 more than a full price offer. How did this happen? It happened because you put all of the potential buyers together in the same room. You "compressed" them. All the emotional, financial, and time pressure was on the buyers. There was absolutely no pressure on you!

## Auctioning

Most of us tend to think about auctioning in one of two ways. The first way we think about auctioning is a Sotheby's or Christie's auction. Usually this involves celebrity memorabilia, art masterpieces, expensive jewels, or huge estate properties. The bids may be made in person, by facsimile, satellite phone, or the Internet. The sophisticated, well heeled, very posh bidders are normally paying new record prices for the auctioned items.

The second way we think about auctioning is the real estate foreclosure auction. The bids are made in person at the auction site, which is typically on the county courthouse steps. Historically this has been where a savvy bidder can purchase a property at 10, 20, or 30 percent or more below market value when properties are not underwater or the market is not crashing.

We are going to show you how to benefit from these two differing perceptions in the auctioning of your investment properties. On the one hand, we will teach you how to obtain a Sotheby's-style auction result with bidders paying top dollar for your property.

On the other hand, we will teach you how to make bidders feel that they can get a great buy at your auction. This is the main reason why most bidders will come to your auction and bid: They think they are going to get a steal of a deal.

## Auction Components

An auction consists of three components: an auctioneer, something to auction, and bidders. We already have the "something" to auction. What we need to talk about is the auctioneer and the bidders. Let's start with the auctioneer. The auctioneer is the person conducting the auction. Who will conduct your auction is the first question you have to answer.

## Who Conducts Your Auction?

You must determine if you or a professional auctioneer should be the auctioneer for your auction. We believe you are the person best suited to be the auctioneer! No one has as big an interest in selling your property for top dollar as you do!

## Qualifications

You have to possess several important qualifications in order to be the auctioneer. To start with the obvious, the auctioneer must be able to talk. When the auctioneer talks the bidders must to be able to understand what is being said.

The auction is about the bidders! A good auctioneer focuses his attention on the bidders. If you can speak, are understood by the people you are speaking to, and can focus your attention on the bidders, then you are qualified to be the auctioneer!

## Special Guidelines

There are special guidelines that we recommend the auctioneer follow. You will guarantee a successful auction if you use all five guidelines. The special guidelines are Connecting, Communicating, Controlling, Compressing, and Using Auction Fever.

**Connecting**   The auctioneer establishes a connection with the bidders. The bidders are assembled in the auction room. It is precisely 8 P.M. You begin. "Welcome to tonight's auction! My name is Liam. I will be your auctioneer this evening. We are about to begin the auction. Before we do please take a moment to review with me how the auction will be conducted."

**Communicating**   The auctioneer is in communication with the bidders. "This is a reserved bid auction. The highest bidder is the winner as long as that bid meets or exceeds the reserved bid. I will recognize your bid when you raise your bidding number above your head. The bidding is over when I say so. The bidding results are final. If you are the winning bidder please see me immediately at the conclusion of the auction. Are there any questions?"

**Controlling**   The auctioneer is in control. The auctioneer must be in control; otherwise you have chaos. Be in control of what? The auctioneer has to be in control of the bidding! The auctioneer may say something like this:

"Your job as bidders is to bid to your hearts' content. My job as auction-eer is to make sure everyone who wants to bid gets the opportunity to bid.

In the event you bid incorrectly, I will be here to get the bidding back on track. For example, if your bid is the same as a previous bid, I will ask you to correct your bid— upward, of course!"

**Compressing**   The auctioneer promotes buyer compression. Remem-ber we said buyer compression brings multiple buyers into a veritable feeding frenzy where the emotional, financial, and time pressure is all on the buyers to bid. The auctioneer must be aware of every bidder and invite interaction between auctioneer and bidders. For example: Let's say we have seven bidders at the auction. Two of the bidders are chomp-ing at the bit.

What does a good auctioneer do to have the other five bidders par-ticipate in the bidding? Ask for bids! "Ladies and gentlemen, as the bid-ding proceeds, I may ask you directly for a bid. I do this to make sure you have the opportunity to bid.

We will open the bidding at $150,000. Do I hear $160,000?" Bidder number 6 bids $160,000. "We have $160,000. Do I hear $170,000?" Bid-der number 4 bids $170,000. "We have $170,000. Do I hear $175,000?" Bidder number 1 bids $175,000. "We have $175,000. Bidder number 5, would you like to make a bid?"

**Using Auction Fever**   The auctioneer encourages auction fever. Let's pick it up from the auctioneer's point of view using our auction from earlier in the chapter. Bidder number 5 is the Pitches and they like your property. The Pitches bid $190,000. Liam, the auctioneer, notices bidder number 3, the Greens, are squirming in their seats and pauses for a mo-ment.

The Greens can't stand it any longer. The Greens bid $195,000. The Pitches decide to make one more bid. They bid $196,000. The Greens bid $199,000. Liam asks the Pitches if they would like to make another bid. The Pitches drop out of the bidding. The Greens are getting excited! Liam asks for more bids.

None are forthcoming. Liam says: "Going once" (for $199,000) ... The Greens can hardly stand it! "Going twice." They are about to get their dream home! They can taste victory. Liam is about to say "Gone! Sold to bidder number 3 for $199,000," when suddenly, bidder number 13 bids $205,000! The Greens' hearts are in their throats. "Who the hell is bid-der number 13?" Liam watches the Greens crane their swollen necks to glare at their rival. "Oh my God!" Bidder number 13 is the Hoppers' cousins, the Mantises!

Liam is watching the Greens' faces, which look dazed and they seem to be having trouble hearing as if their heads were under water. The Greens hear Liam intone: "Going once . . . going twice . . ." Liam watches Mrs. Green elbow Mr. Green in the ribs. She looks like she is about to whisper but instead screams in his ear, "Bid!" Mr. Green, shocked by the noise in his ear, jumps up and blurts outs, "$209,000!" Liam says, "Going once. Going twice. Gone! Sold to bidder number 3 for $209,000!" The auctioneer has encouraged auction fever.

### Use a Professional Auctioneer

There may be several reasons for you to have a professional auctioneer conduct your auction. We are going to go over six of these reasons with you. Besides your properties, your two most valuable assets are time and money. These two assets and how you want to allocate them will help you determine whether to have your property auctioned by a professional auctioneer.

Remember to check to see if your region has a licensing requirement for professional auctioneers.

**Time**   The first reason to have a professional auctioneer conduct your auction is because you don't want to allocate the time to conduct it yourself. You are already too busy. Never mind the fact that you can save big bucks if you do it yourself. Your time is so precious to you that you would rather pay the money than spend the time. Besides, when would you have the time to make the phone calls, set up the meetings, and put together an auction team?

**Special Circumstances**   The second reason to have a professional auctioneer auction your property is because of special circumstances. Maybe you are too ill or incapacitated. Maybe you are getting a divorce. Maybe you hate teams and hate being on a team. Maybe you feel very uncomfortable sharing the decision making process with anyone else including your spouse. Maybe you are a mess at the time! We all have our strong points and our weak points. It is okay to be unable to do everything yourself in every situation all the time. If you feel like you just can not do it yourself then hire a professional auctioneer to do it for you using this book as the guideline for what you want!

**Out of Town**    The third reason to use a professional auctioneer is that you live out of town. In this situation, the logistics of some auction types make auctioning difficult to do yourself. However, with a careful choice of auction type you may still be able to auction your property yourself with the help of your auction team.

**Ginormous Property**    The fourth reason to hire a professional auctioneer is that you have a ginormous property. Usually the bidders on this caliber of property would be accustomed to dealing with professionals. However, some may find it refreshing to deal with you as the owner. The point is, just having a huge property does not preclude you from auctioning your property yourself.

**Hugo the Ego**    The fifth reason to engage a professional auctioneer is that you choose to be like a character we will call Hugo the Ego. Hugo the Ego's personality needs the ego gratification of being able to say, "I am having Sotheby's do it!" Hey, as long as life can be these days, it is still too short to worry about what other people think! If it makes you happy to be like Hugo the Ego then go for it!

**Alone**    The sixth reason to have a professional auctioneer auction your property is that you cannot do an auction by yourself. Let's say you have tried to get a team together, but for whatever reason you have not been able to make it happen. You will need to call in a professional auctioneer.

**Cost**    What does it cost to have a professional auctioneer conduct your auction? The answer is, like real estate commissions, it is negotiable! The good news is that many professional auctioneers work off of a Buyer's Premium. Instead of the owner or seller paying the auctioneering fees the buyer or bidder pays the fees.

Typically the Buyer's Premium is a percentage of the winning bid. Let's look at an example.

If the Greens have the winning bid of $209,000 for your property, you want the whole $209,000 right? If you conducted your own auction that is what you would receive. A professional auctioneer may charge 5 percent of the sales price. In this case that would be $10,450. If you paid that, it would be equivalent to your paying a real estate commission.

### *Buyer's Premium*

However, if there is a Buyer's Premium involved you would pay nothing and the Greens would pay the $10,450. Depending on whether you have a ginormous property the auctioneer may have a Buyer's Premium requirement *and* charge you, the owner, a fee. Be sure you are clear on what the financial expectations are.

For example, let's say you have a Texas-size ranch with the acreage to go with it. You retain the services of a professional auctioneer. The auctioneer spends money on advertising and promoting your ranch for auction. The champagne and catered open houses have cost a pretty penny.

You have set a reserved bid requirement for your auction. The auction occurs and the high bidder does not meet your reserved bid. You do not have to sell your ranch. The auctioneer will want to be paid something. Have a contract in place that spells out how much the auctioneer can spend and expect to be reimbursed by you.

## Bidders

Next we have the bidders. The bidders are the most important component of your auction. Bidders are buyers. No bidders . . . no buyers . . . no sale! Your number one priority is attracting bidders to your auction.

We are going to show you how to attract bidders to your auction. We will show you how to advertise your auction. You will learn how to write an auction announcement to attract bidders.

Once you have bidders at your auction you want them to buy your property. We will tell you how to have the bidders at your auction buy your property for top dollar. Putting these components together correctly is the way to guarantee you will have a successful auction.

## Advertising Your Auction

While advertising your property for auction is different from advertising your property for sale, there are some parallels. We suggest you create an auction announcement and a Property Fact Pack including a property fact sheet, disclosure statement, and auction information sheet for your property. When people respond to your auction announcement you can offer them the Property Fact Pack.

### *Auction Announcement*

We will describe what you should include in your auction announcement and then give you a sample auction announcement classified ad. Your auction announcement begins by announcing the auctioning of your property, gives the address of your property, and when and where the auction will take place.

It will also let prospective bidders know when the property is available for preview, what type of auction it will be, provide a brief description of your property, and instructions on who to contact and where to obtain further information.

You will notice that we said nothing about price or terms. Your auction announcement is designed to intrigue people. You want to give them enough information to arouse their curiosity so they will call you. If you give them too much information in the auction announcement they might eliminate your property from further consideration without your having a chance to pique their interest.

## Fun

We have observed that the more fun, intrigue, and curiosity you can create for people the better the response you will receive. Remember that unlike the traditional real estate selling adage "it only takes one buyer," many buyers (bidders) are your goal for your auction.

**Auction Announcement!**

Announcing the auctioning
of the property located at
1600 Pennsylvania Avenue
Washington, D.C.
April 1, 2009 at 8 P.M.
on the premises.
Property available for preview

Monday through Friday
from 10 A.M. to 4 P.M.
March 27 to March 31, 2009.
This is a reserved bid auction.
The property is a large, antebellum two story.
Work, play, and living areas.
Fenced with excellent security.
For further information contact
the General Services Administration
at 1-800 BAILOUT.

### *When to Advertise?*

When should you run your auction announcement? That depends on what type of auction you are conducting. We recommend that you advertise for live auctions on the Friday, Saturday, and Sunday of the weekend before the actual weekend of your auction. We recommend that you advertise a sealed bid auction (see Chapter 13) on Friday, Saturday, and Sunday for the four weeks leading up to the day you open the sealed bids.

### *Where To Advertise?*

We recommend you run your auction announcement in the real estate classifieds for the area where your property would normally be advertised. That way the people who are already shopping your location will find your auction announcement. If you have access to the Internet we recommend you explore what is available to you at the time you are reading this book.

Be creative in considering where to advertise your auction. Use everything from high tech (Internet, online classifieds) to high touch (you know . . . talk to people) to get the word out. The name of the game for a successful auction is exposure!

### *Property Fact Pack*

As mentioned earlier, the Property Fact Pack should include the property fact sheet, disclosure statement, and auction information sheet.

These should be as attractive as possible working within your budget. Remember you are marketing your property to your potential bidders and you want as many to show up for the auction as possible!

## Property Fact Sheet

What should the property fact sheet include? It should contain as much information about the property as possible. How many bedrooms and bathrooms? How many living areas? Any special features such as a swimming pool, hot tub, or tennis court?

What kind of heat? Do you have central air? Hardwood floors? How many car garages? Any new appliances or improvements? Recently painted? New roof? Trees, view, privacy, lot size? What attracted or interested you about this property when you bought it?

## Disclosure Statement

Include a disclosure statement. A disclosure statement is a listing of what is included with the property and what is not included with the property. Is there anything that doesn't work or is in need of repair? Are you located in a flood zone? Is there a toxic waste site down the street?

The point we are making about the disclosure statement is that you must disclose everything you are aware of with regard to your property. Our experience has shown us that prospective buyers (bidders) can handle anything you disclose up front with absolutely no problem.

In fact, they want to know so that their offers (bids) can reflect anything that needs to be taken care of on your property. It is when the buyer finds out after the fact that there are problems that the proverbial Texas cow pies hit the fan.

## Auction Information

The third item that your Property Fact Pack *must* include is your auction information sheet. Your auction information sheet will specify the type of auction you are conducting, the rules for the auction, how to bid, and the form of acceptable payment. The auction information sheet should also include an auction registration form.

In the next chapter, we will introduce you to the types of auctions you might consider to sell your property in a crashing real estate market. These nine auction types can be mixed and matched. Your goal is to have a successful auction.

# CHAPTER 13

# Types of Auctions

There are many types of auctions. We are going to talk about nine auctions in this chapter. You may find that you want to mix and match parts of two, three, or more of these auctions for your successful auction.

After you have decided on the type of auction you are going to use, we will talk about your auction team. You may decide to put an auction team together to assist you in conducting your auction.

And finally, we will show you how to prepare your property for auction. What do you do to the property and when do you do it? What about the day of the auction? Should you make repairs? Stay tuned for these and other answers.

By the way, this is a good time to mention that it is legal to auction your own property in all 50 states, the District of Columbia, and Canada. If you live elsewhere, please check your local requirements or restrictions. If you are going to have someone conduct your auction other than yourself, an immediate family member, or a trustee separate from control of the property, your region may require that the auctioneer be licensed. Be sure to check the laws regarding auctions in whatever country your property is located. Many countries around the world do allow auctions.

## Types of Auctions

We are going to talk about a foreclosure auction, a weekend auction, an absolute auction, a reserve bid auction, a spot bid auction, a Dutch auction, a sealed bid auction, a Sotheby's auction, and an Internet auction.

## Foreclosure/Weekend/Absolute

The first three auctions to discuss are the foreclosure auction, the weekend auction, and the absolute auction. These three are all used for special circumstances, though the weekend auction really could be used for any reason.

A foreclosure auction is conducted by the county sheriff or representative of the lender on the courthouse steps, usually on a weekday morning. In a foreclosure auction the lender makes the first bid with a credit bid for the amount of principal, interest, advertising costs, auction fees, and auction expenses the lender is owed or has incurred. There is no cash required on the lender's part, hence the term credit bid. Any subsequent bidders must have cash or a cash equivalent to make a bid.

A weekend auction is exactly what it implies. You have your property available for previewing by interested bidders only on Saturday and Sunday. The auctioning is conducted on Sunday evening. Wow! Here today, gone tomorrow!

An absolute auction (no, this one is not about vodka) alerts the bidders to the fact that the auctioned item will be sold to the highest bidder. The owner must sell to the highest bidder even if the owner is unhappy with the bid and considers the bid too low. This is normally used in times of dire need such as legal time constraints pursuant to some sort of misfortune.

## Reserve Bid/Spot Bid/Dutch

The next three auctions to discuss are the reserve bid auction, the spot bid auction, and the Dutch auction. All three of these auctions encourage the bidders to bid their highest possible bid.

A reserve bid auction allows the owner to set a reserve price for his property. The reserve price is determined prior to the auction beginning and is undisclosed to the bidders. The bidders are encouraged to bid high or risk losing the opportunity to have a winning bid. If the highest bid does not meet or exceed the owner's reserve bid the property owner does not have to sell his property.

Spot bid auction has the assembled bidders write their bids on a card. This is a one-shot chance for the bidders to win. The bidders are forced to bid their top bid immediately in hopes of winning the bid. The bidding cards are collected. The auctioneer examines the bids and determines the highest bidder. The highest bidder is then declared the winner!

A Dutch auction refers to the way the Dutch have bought and sold flowers for hundreds of years. Due to the variety, color, quality, and quantity of flowers coming to the market and the presence of multiple buyers, a Dutch auction may produce more than one winning bidder.

In a Dutch auction the auctioneer starts at a high price and works backward until a bid is made. Because we are talking about only one property there can be only one winner. The first bid wins. There can only be one first bid. The bidders are forced to bid higher than they may have expected or risk not being the first bid and therefore losing the property!

## Sealed Bid/Sotheby's/Internet

The last three auctions to discuss are the sealed bid auction, the Sotheby's auction, and the Internet auction.

A sealed bid auction means all bids are made beforehand and sealed in an envelope. The bids are then unsealed on a designated date and the first submitted highest bid is declared the winner. The federal government's Department of Housing and Urban Development (HUD) conducts sealed bid auctions. This is another one-shot bid situation so the bidders have to put their best bid forward or risk losing the property.

A Sotheby's auction normally involves expensive auction items and attracts more affluent bidders. Sotheby's is an upscale auction house in New York. We are using Sotheby's as an example of a professional auctioneer. The auctioneer opens the bidding to the floor of prequalified bidders and the bidding continues until the top bid wins. This is quite the posh affair!

An Internet auction. A host of possible online real estate auction sites are available for you to use. Just research on the net for possibilities and find one you like best. Some of the preparations for an Internet auction are similar to the preparations for a live auction. There are some obvious and not so obvious differences. You still have to prepare your home for an Internet auction. You will have to perform the repairs that sell your property. These are the same repairs you would make for a live auction. You will have to create an auction announcement to post on the Internet. You may decide to have an auction team. You have to decide what type of auction you are going to have.

No need to have bidder's paddles. No need to have an auctioneer. You will want to turn on all the lights and have a fire in the fireplace when you take pictures of your property with your digital camera to include in your Internet property fact sheet.

## Other Types of Auctions

There are certainly plenty of other types of auctions. Some are defined by how the auction is conducted such as a silent auction. Some are defined by what is being auctioned such as an antiques auction. We want to give you a taste of the types of auctions so you can get a feel for how prevalent auctioning really is.

An analogy would be after you start driving a new car you begin to notice your make, model, and even color wherever you go. Before you bought your new car you may have hardly noticed any on the road. Auctioning is the same way. Once you get interested in auctioning you start to see auctions and auctioning information everywhere.

Every type of auction works. This is very good news. What this means is whatever auction type you choose to use to auction your property, it will work! All you have to do is become familiar with the auctions we recommend and pick an auction that fits your inclinations, time availability, and budget.

## Picking an Auction

How do you choose the auction that is best for you? You may want to try what we will call "vanilla," "chocolate," or "strawberry." We will briefly walk you through three different auction scenarios. We will build on the nine auctions by mixing and matching them. This is how we came up with our three "flavors" for you to taste.

## Vanilla Auction

A vanilla auction combines a foreclosure auction and a weekend auction. How does a vanilla auction work? Two weekends before your auction you sit down and make your auction plan. This includes determining the market value of your property if you have not already done so. It also includes figuring out who should be on your auction team if you plan to have one.

You advertise the auction the Friday, Saturday, and Sunday before the actual weekend of your auction. During the week before your auction you prepare your property for the auction. On the Saturday and Sunday of your auction weekend you hold an open house from noon to five o'clock each day to allow buyers to preview your property. At five o'clock on Sunday afternoon you close down the open house. Between five o'clock and seven o'clock you will set up the auction.

You will reopen for the auction at seven o'clock. From seven o'clock until the action begins at eight o'clock you will greet and meet your guests (bidders). At eight o'clock the auction begins.

### Vanilla Variations

Some of the variations for the vanilla auction include adding elements from an absolute auction, a reserve bid auction, or a spot bid auction. Let's start with the absolute auction.

Even though in an absolute auction the highest bidder wins and you must sell the property to that highest bidder no matter how low the price, you may be happy to find that holding an absolute auction attracts more bidders. However, you may be unhappy with the amount of the highest bidder's bid. Let's see how we can take care of the absolute auction problem by using a reserve bid auction.

In a reserve bid auction you set a minimum price for your home and unless the highest bidder meets or exceeds your reserve bid, you do not have to sell your property. Problem solved. So, what about the spot bid auction?

In a spot bid auction the bidders write their bids on a special card. Each bidder only gets one bid so they are forced to bid their top price. The bids are collected and the auctioneer determines the highest bidder. The winner is then announced.

## Chocolate Auction

A chocolate auction is our version of a Dutch auction. (Dutch chocolate?) As we said earlier, a Dutch auction refers to how the Dutch have bought and sold flowers for hundreds of years. A chocolate auction is set up in the same manner as a vanilla auction. The difference between the two lies in how the auctions are conducted.

A vanilla auction is conducted like a foreclosure auction in that the bidding starts out low and then moves higher. In a chocolate auction the bidding starts out high and moves lower. Whichever bidder makes the first bid is the winner.

### *Chocolate Variations*

Some of the variations for a chocolate auction include an absolute auction and a reserve bid auction. As stated before, even though in an absolute auction the highest bidder wins, which in this Dutch auction case would be the first bidder, you must sell the property to that highest bidder no matter how low the price. However, if you use a reserve bid auction you set a minimum price for your home and unless the first bidder in the Dutch auction meets or exceeds your reserve bid, you do not have to sell your property.

## Strawberry Auction

A strawberry auction is a combination of a sealed bid auction and a reserve bid auction. In a sealed bid auction the bidders will send their bids in by mail. A monetary deposit in an acceptable form specified by the auction announcement must accompany the bid. Otherwise the bid will not be considered. This deposit can range from 1 percent to 25 percent of the bid amount. The highest bidder with the earliest postmark is the winner.

As previously stated, in a reserve bid auction you set a minimum price for your property and unless the highest bidder meets or exceeds your reserve bid, you do not have to sell your property.

Thirty days before your auction (in this case, the date you have set to open the bids) you sit down and make your auction plan. This includes determining the market value of your home and preparing your home for auction. You advertise your auction on Friday, Saturday, and Sunday for the next four weeks. You have your property available for preview by appointment during the week and hold an open house on Saturday and Sunday from noon to five o'clock, which should give anyone interested in your property time to come by and take a look.

As you receive bids by mail marked "Sealed Bid," arrange them by postmark rather than by when you receive them. On the date you have specified for the opening of the bids remember to start with the earliest postmark. If you have two or more bids that are the highest bid, the bid with the earliest postmark is the winner. You must immediately return the deposits to all the unsuccessful bidders.

### Strawberry Variations

Some of the variations for a strawberry auction include adding elements from an absolute auction and a spot bid auction. With the absolute auction variation to your strawberry auction you would inform the bidders that you are selling your home to the highest bidder, period. No minimums and no reserves. Winner takes all. As you open the sealed bids, the property goes to the first posted highest bidder.

With the spot bid variation to your strawberry auction you would have the bidders phone in their best bid during a designated two-hour window. Whoever has the highest bid at the earliest time would be the winner as long as it meets your reserve bid.

### Endless Possibilities

As you can see there are endless possibilities in combining auction variations. Be creative and have fun with it. Whether you are a homeowner looking to make the most on the sale of your home or an investor looking to add more fun to your investing adventure, auctioning will be whatever you make of it! Now, who are you going to invite to play with you?

## Auction Team

You may decide to put together an auction team. Who should you choose? Before we can answer this question we need to tell you what positions are available on your team. It is possible to have one person fill more than one position. We recommend that you have at least two people on your team. Three or four people would be better. A husband and wife team; you, your significant other, and a friend team; you and your two siblings team; you and your partner(s); you and someone else is the point.

## Auctioneer

The auctioneer is the first position for you to fill on your auction team. Now, we know that each one of you has some picture in your mind of what an auctioneer looks and sounds like. This image ranges from Earl Elocution, who enunciates exquisitely, to Rodeo Randy, who talks so fast you have no idea what he is saying. (We can say that because we are Texans.)

We believe you will be able to conduct your own auction. In the previous chapter, we gave you the qualifications and special guidelines you need so you will be able to auction your property for top dollar. What we will say here is that the auctioneer is the premier player of your team.

## Bidders' Buddy

The second member of your auction team is the person we call the "bidders' buddy." The bidders' buddy is the person who takes care of the bidders. The bidders' buddy greets each bidder as he or she arrives and gives them the auction information sheet and the auction registration form.

Now the bidders know (or are reminded from having earlier read the auction announcement) what kind of auction is being conducted, how to bid, and what form of payment is acceptable. The bidders' buddy makes the bidders comfortable by answering any questions they may have about the auction.

## Money Magnate

The next position on your team is the money magnate. (How many of you thought it was money magnet? That name would work, too!) The money magnate verifies the bidders' funds, obtains their pertinent financial data, and gives the winner instructions for closing the transaction.

## Preparations Pasha

The final position on your team is what we call the preparations pasha. The preparations pasha is in charge of all the preparations for the auction. This person handles everything from A to Z. From developing the auction plan to writing the auction announcement to placing advertising, preparing your property, holding the open house and setting up the auction, the preparations pasha is the captain of your team. So, who should do what?

## Who Should Do What?

Let us say that you, your spouse, and your adult daughter are the auction team. At your auction planning meeting the three of you look at the four positions we have described in this chapter: auctioneer, bidders' buddy, money magnate, and preparations pasha. You each have your strengths. Flip a coin to see who gets to select first.

Let's say you win the coin toss. You choose to be the auctioneer. Your spouse wants to be the preparations pasha. Your daughter is ecstatic to be the bidders' buddy. Great! What does that leave? Who is going to be the money magnate?

Who is the best with handling financial details and who is going to have the most fun in that position? If your spouse or your daughter is not going to have fun being the money magnate, then you do it or find another player who wants to assume the role. Each of these positions is an important one. Your successful auction depends on your successful team.

### Additional Positions

In addition to the four main positions we have described, we suggest you consider the following additional positions. These are positions that will require additional bodies. They can be filled by friends or family.

The next position would be the parking valet. This person or persons would be in front of your property to direct guests where to park. We recommend that your parking valet actually park the guest's cars. The next position(s) would be kitchen staff. These individuals would help prepare refreshments for your bidders. You will also need helpers to serve your guests between their arrival at 7 P.M. and the beginning of your auction at 8 P.M. Remember to think about after the auction cleanup!

## Preparing Your Property for Auction

How do you prepare your property for auction? The answer is you do everything you would do to prepare your property for showing. What about the day of the auction? Let's start with the basics and what you should do if you were going to sell your property yourself or through a broker. We will draw on our decades of experience as real estate brokers and consultants helping sellers to prepare their properties for sale.

We can tell you almost without exception that you will be like every property owner we have ever met. You will proudly tell us about your plans for improving your property. You are planning on adding another bathroom. Or perhaps you are planning on adding another bedroom, or a _____ (fill in the blank). Stop! Don't do it. It takes too much time and too much money. Do not bother!

# Repairs

Next you will tell us about the repairs that you have been meaning to get around to but you have just been too busy to make. What repairs should you make and what repairs should you forget about? Listen up!

Repairing obvious problems makes your property more salable to a greater number of bidders. If your property has damage that needs repair and you are able to make the repair at a reasonable cost, then we recommend you make the repair.

We have found that the increased price your property commands more than makes up for the cost of the repairs. We will mention one caveat here with regard to repairs. *Do not attempt to conceal problems by making poor or temporary cosmetic repairs.*

Your region may require you to make extensive disclosures to the buyer of your home. Intentional errors or omissions may leave you liable to the buyer for "actual and punitive damages" (the legalese). For a more extensive treatment of this subject, including a very easy to use repairs worksheet, see our book *How To Sell Your Home Without A Broker*, fourth edition, by Bill Carey, Chantal Howell Carey, and Suzanne Kiffmann, John Wiley & Sons, Inc.

# Staging

Finally, you will knowingly tell us all the staging you are going to undertake to make your property more attractive to prospective buyers. You will depersonalize the house. You will rearrange the furnishings. You will have popcorn popping or cookies baking while showing your home. You will have soothing music playing throughout the property. You will turn all the lights on inside the property even though it is broad daylight. Bravo! These are all excellent ideas.

Anything you do to enhance your property's attractiveness is like money in the bank. Remember that attractiveness is in the eyes, nose, and ears of the beholder. Now that your property is ready to show, we will tell you how to set up for the auction. On Sunday afternoon you spend from five o'clock to seven o'clock setting up your auction. What do you do? Complete each item on the Top 10 Preparations list.

**Top 10 Preparations**

1. Park your cars in the garage or preferably down the street.
2. Turn on all the lights inside and outside your home.
3. Put on classical or smooth jazz music at low volume.
4. Make popcorn or cookies.
5. Have coffee, tea, water, and soft drinks available.
6. Close off the bedrooms.
7. Set the temperature between 68 and 72 degrees.
8. Light a fire in the fireplace.
9. Brief auction team and have them in their positions by 6:30 P.M.
10. Allow guests in starting exactly at seven o'clock.

The purpose of the Top 10 Preparations list, besides serving as a reminder for you, is to ensure that you take care of your guests. This list represents the minimum that should be done. Feel free to upgrade to a level above what would be considered the neighborhood norm, such as serving champagne and catered hors d'oeuvres, for example. People who are made to feel special and feel your property is special will want to live in your property. When your guests feel this way, they will feel like bidding.

Let's take a closer look at the Top 10 Preparations list.

1. Park your cars in the garage or down the street. This creates parking for your guests. By providing a parking valet you make the guests feel special. Your property and your auction must also be special.
2. Turn on all the lights inside and outside your property. This makes your property stand out. Lights convey an open and festive mood. Your guests will feel like they are attending a gala of some sort. They are, aren't they?
3. Put on classical or smooth jazz music at low volume. Again, you are going for mood. You are creating a posh environment. You are showing that you respect your guests.
4. Make popcorn or cookies. Americans associate the smell of popcorn with going to the movies. People go to the movies for fun and excitement. You want your guests to have fun and be excited at your auction. If you are going more for the secure, homey feel, you may want to make cookies instead.

5. Have coffee, tea, water, and soft drinks available. By being a good host you help guarantee a successful auction. When you take care of your bidders, your bidders will take care of you.

6. Close off the bedrooms. This signals to your guests that while they are welcome to your property, tonight is about business.

7. Have the temperature set between 68 and 72 degrees. This is very important. If your guests are too hot or too cold this may distract them from bidding.

8. Light a fire in the fireplace. A fire in the fireplace is worth a thousand words and thousands of dollars to you. Warmth, happiness, dreams, comfort, love, family, and joy are just some of the positive feelings, emotions, and thoughts that human beings associate with a fire in the hearth.

9. Auction team briefed and in position by 6:30. Everyone on your auction team knows the game plan. What is the timeline? What is their job for the evening going to be?

10. Allow guests in starting exactly at seven o'clock. You must start to let people in exactly at seven o'clock. The guests can be late. You can never be late. If the guests are early have a place where they can wait.

Do you feel that you will be able to prepare your property for showing? Do you feel good about your being able to prepare your property for auction? Are you ready for the next step? In the next chapter we will discuss the who, when, and how of your auction.

# CHAPTER 14

# The Who, When, and How of Your Auction

This chapter is about the who, when, and how of your auction. Near the end of this chapter, we have also included some auction precautions. Starting with the who, we will share with you our observations about how people react when buying the biggest ticket item of their lives. What is the biggest ticket item in most of all our lives? Real estate! And, for most people real estate means our homes.

Owning your own home is a big part of the American Dream. Where there are dreams, there are emotions and feelings. The bigger the dreams the bigger the emotions and feelings. Whenever dreams, emotions, and feelings surface, it seems reason and logic are out the door. So what does this have to do with auctioning your property? Everything!

## Retail Buyers Buying at Your Auction

Retail buyers are your target market for buying at your auction. We have said that wholesale buyers will be attracted to your auction because of their association of auctions with foreclosures. Wholesale buyers are looking for a good deal. However, a retail buyer who has attached his or her dreams, emotions, and feelings to your auction property as a potential home will pay a higher price than any wholesale buyer.

## What Retail Buyers Say They Can Afford

Retail buyers tell us all the time that they can only afford a home in a certain price range. The Goldtrees told us they were looking in a price range of $300,000 to $325,000. We showed the Goldtrees property priced as high as $400,000. Lo and behold, we found them a property that they fell in love with.

The property was on the market for $389,000. We wrote and presented an offer for them for $355,000. This was after much hemming and hawing on the Goldtrees' part because they were concerned that the home was out of their price range. Before we presented the Goldtrees' offer, we were told another offer was coming in. The sellers wanted both offers presented before they would make a decision.

### *Bidding War*

Guess what happened? We became involved in a bidding war! (Remember when we told you that every real estate transaction is really like an auction?) The sellers made a counteroffer of $389,000, full price, to both offers. That was a very smart move on the sellers' part.

Whichever buyer responded first with the highest counteroffer would get the property. When we got with our clients they were panicked to learn someone else was trying to "steal their dream home." They insisted on immediately offering $415,000 to the seller to make sure that they outbid the other buyers. Our offer was accepted by the seller. The Goldtrees were ecstatic!

Later on, we found out that the other buyers rejected the sellers' counteroffer. All the Goldtrees needed to do was accept the sellers' original $389,000 price. Out of their "love" for the home and their "panic" that they were going to lose it, the Goldtrees paid at least $26,000 more than necessary for the property. They also paid $90,000 more than they told us was the upper limit of their price range. Are you getting this?

## The Buying of Homes Is Ultimately Controlled by Emotions

These emotions and feelings run the gamut from the positive (hope, love, happiness, ecstasy, joy, dreams) to the negative (fear, loss, remorse, panic, pain, nightmares). All these emotions and feelings are going to be present at your auction. Who buys property at real estate auctions? Emotional people do, that's who!

You *must* create an environment at your auction that is conducive to the buyers becoming emotionally involved in the bidding. At the same time *you* must remain emotionally uninvolved in the bidding. Are you willing to create the environment at your auction for auction fever to break out?

### *Auction Fever*

What is this auction fever stuff again? Auction fever is a condition that overcomes some people when they are participating in an auction. It is caused by a convergence of positive and negative emotions as the bidding progresses. How does this apply when it comes to the auctioning of your property?

The fever reaches its peak as all the hopes, dreams, and happiness associated by the bidders with living in your/their property collide with the fears, nightmares, and panic of not living in your/their property.

The symptoms of auction fever are shallow breathing, flushing, churning stomach, eyes glazing over, and chest pounding. Bidders in the grip of auction fever tend to keep bidding. In fact, such bidders are the winning bidder in many auctions. Sometimes the only cure for auction fever is to be the winning bidder!

Our point is you should expect bidders at your auction to have auction fever. You don't cause it. You can't prevent it. You just want to encourage it. Auction fever has to run its course. Auction fever can have very positive results. You can auction your property off in a short time period and receive top dollar. The winning bidder can be thrilled with his new home.

Studying people and what motivates them will help you understand how to structure your auction. Auctioning your property is not rocket science. You now need to figure out when to conduct your auction and, of course, there is the necessity of showing the property before the auction.

## Showing Your Property

Before you can conduct your auction you have to show your property to potential bidders. The result of a successful showing is a potential bidder comes to your auction and bids. We are going to share with you some of our ideas for showing your property.

Be helpful and attentive when you are showing your property *and* give people space to check things out for themselves. Point out the wonderful features as a potential bidder experiences the benefits available in your property. A feature of your property is a fireplace. A benefit is when a person experiences the sight, sound, smell, and warmth of the fire in your fireplace.

The Top 10 Preparations list from Chapter 13 is a good place to start. Park your cars in the garage or down the street. Turn on all the lights inside your home. Put on classical or smooth jazz music at low volume. Have the temperature set between 68 and 72 degrees. Make popcorn or cookies. Have coffee, tea, water, and soft drinks available. Light a fire in the fireplace.

When the guests arrive, have them sign in with their name, address, and telephone number. This is smart for security reasons as it gives you a record of who has been in your property. It also makes it easy for you to do follow-up.

After the guests have viewed the property and are getting ready to leave, remember to ask if they would like a Property Fact Pack. If you give them the Property Fact Pack when they arrive they will be distracted by the paperwork and some of the impact of seeing your property will be lost.

We suggest that after the showing, you sit down with an interested person and go over the Property Fact Pack. Do this at the kitchen table (this creates a business rather than social tone). While this is business, do invite the prospect to have a cup of coffee and some popcorn or cookies to help create rapport.

## Best Days/Best Time

When is the best time to conduct your auction? What is the best day to conduct your auction? We recommend you conduct your auction on a Saturday or Sunday evening at eight o'clock. However, we suggest that in your auction plan you select the day and time that is best for you. Once you have decided to auction your property, your first order of business is to meet with your auction team and create your auction plan. The auction schedule is the backbone of your auction plan.

Regarding timing: Be flexible. Internet bidders can make bids at every moment of every day from anywhere they are. If you bought this book today and want to auction your property tomorrow an Internet auction would be the way to go. If you are conducting a "live" auction we recommend you pick the date and time for your auction and then work backward to design your auction schedule.

## Auction Schedule: Vanilla

Let's say you pick Saturday September 26, 2009, at eight o'clock in the evening for your vanilla auction. Working backward you schedule Friday, September 25 through Monday, September 21 from 10 A.M. to 4 P.M. for prospective purchasers to preview the property. Your auction announcement will run in the newspaper and Internet on Sunday, Saturday, and Friday September 20, 19, 18. Your preparations pasha will place the ad on Thursday, September 17.

Your bidders' buddy will confirm all auction paperwork is completed on Wednesday, September 16. Your money magnate will produce the bidders' funds and auction registration forms on Tuesday, September 15. Your preparations pasha will supervise the preparation of you property for auction on Monday, September 14. On Sunday, September 13, you and your auction team will meet to make your auction plan.

## Auction Schedule: Chocolate

What about a chocolate auction? We have said a chocolate auction is set up the same way as a vanilla auction. You may use the same auction schedule as the vanilla auction for your chocolate auction.

## Auction Schedule: Strawberry

What about a strawberry auction? We said a strawberry auction was a sealed bid auction. We recommended thirty days from planning the Auction to opening the Bids. If we plan to open the bids on Saturday, September 26, 2009, at eight o'clock in the evening, then we would need to start the process on Thursday, August 27.

We suggested a variation to the strawberry auction, which was adding elements of the spot bid auction. Rather than bidders submitting their bids by mail or e-mail, with the spot bid variation to your strawberry auction you would have the bidders phone in their one bid during a designated two-hour window.

Whoever had the highest bid at the earliest time would be the winner. In our example, you would specify that the bidders could submit their bids between six o'clock and eight o'clock the evening of September 26. At one minute past eight you would call the winning bidder and offer your congratulations.

### Auction Schedule: Sotheby's

When do you conduct a Sotheby's auction? Have it whenever you want. Seriously, if you are retaining a professional auctioneer, you and the auctioneer will work together to plan the best time to conduct your auction.

### Auction Schedule: Internet

When do you conduct an Internet auction? The first answer is anytime. The second answer is whenever you are ready.

## How to Conduct Your Auction

We are going to show you how to conduct a vanilla auction and a chocolate auction.

### Vanilla Auction

You may recall that a vanilla auction is a combination of a foreclosure auction and a weekend auction. We are going to take you through your vanilla auction from seven o'clock when you open the door and invite your guests to come inside until eight o'clock when the auctioneer says, "Ladies and gentlemen, may I have your attention please? Welcome to tonight's auction!" This is the hour to build fun and excitement into your auction.

Your auction team is in position by 6:30. Your parking valet has greeted guests at the curb, offered to park their cars, and invited them to proceed to the front door.

**7 P.M.** At seven o'clock Bud, the bidders' buddy, opens the door and greets the arriving guests. Bud makes a name tag for each guest that includes both the first and last name. Bud gives each guest an auction registration form and instructs each one on how to complete it.

After the guest has completed the auction registration, Bud gives each one the auction information and then introduces the guest to Buck, the money magnate. Buck goes over the auction registration form and obtains bidder financial information from the guest. Buck then gives the guest a bidder's paddle with the bidder's number on it.

Meanwhile Posh, the preparations pasha, has the popcorn popping or cookies baking, the coffee brewing, and the other beverages ready to be served. The fire is burning in the fireplace. The classical or smooth jazz music is playing. All the lights have been turned on inside and outside the home. (Do this even if it is still light outside!)

The temperature is between 68 and 72 degrees. All bedroom doors have been closed. Make sure you have a designated guest bathroom available. With all the fun and excitement you may be surprised how often the guest bathroom is used in such a short period of time!

**7:15 P.M.** After the guest has completed his auction registration, Buck will direct him back to Bud. Guests will continue arriving right up till the last minute. The sequence of what the guest does will remain the same. Only the timing will change for the later arriving guests.

Bud will answer any questions the guests may have regarding the auction information or plans for the evening. At this point Posh and staff begin serving guests popcorn or cookies and beverages. The initial paperwork is out of the way and now is the time to have the guests get excited and have fun. No guests are served refreshments unless they are wearing a name tag.

**7:30 P.M.** As the guests are mingling, Bud circulates and introduces them to each other using their first names. This is a crucial part of the evening. You want people to talk and get to know one another before the auction. This gives each bidder a chance to size up the competition. It is Bud's job to ask the guests what dreams, hopes, and feelings they have about living in your property after they win the bidding.

**7:45 P.M.**   At 7:45 P.M., you or whoever is serving as the auctioneer on your team, make your entrance. Bud will introduce you to the guests. "Ladies and gentlemen, please allow me to introduce your auctioneer for this evening, Liam O'Rourke."

You or Liam will welcome the guests and let them know that you will be starting the auction exactly at eight o'clock. You will mingle with the guests and ask them about their hopes, dreams, and feelings with regard to your property.

You and Bud are doing this to encourage the guests to become more emotionally involved with the property. That they are there is our evidence that the guests have already developed an emotional attachment to your property. Remember, we buy real estate emotionally. Reason and logic are in the service of our emotions.

Music, an inviting fire in the fireplace, the smell and taste of popcorn, cookies, and coffee, all this contributes to positive feelings in your guests. From the moment the guests drive up, your purpose is to create an environment of excitement and fun.

As eight o'clock approaches, Bud will usher the guests to the auction room. We recommend you have folding chairs set up in an arc around the area where the auctioneer is going to stand. When all the guests have been seated with their bidding paddles in hand, the auctioneer will again be introduced by Bud and the auction is set to begin. "Ladies and gentlemen, this is the moment you have all been waiting for. I am going to bring Liam O'Rourke to the front of the room to start the auction."

**8 P.M.**   The auctioneer says, "Ladies and gentlemen, may I have your attention please? Welcome to tonight's auction! My name is Liam O'Rourke. I will be your auctioneer this evening. We are about to begin the auction. Before we do, please take a moment to review with me how the auction will be conducted. This is a reserve bid auction. The highest bidder is the winner as long as that bid meets or exceeds the reserve bid.

"I will recognize your bid when you raise your bidding number above your head. The bidding is over when I say so. The bidding results are final. If you are the winning bidder please see Buck (the money magnate) immediately at the conclusion of the auction. Are there any questions? We will open the bidding at $150,000. Do I hear $160,000?"

### *Chocolate Auction*

A chocolate auction is set up in the same manner as a vanilla auction. The chocolate auction will be the same as the vanilla auction right up to the time the auctioneer introduces himself at eight o'clock. After that everything changes.

The difference between a chocolate auction and a vanilla auction lies in how the auction is conducted. In a chocolate auction, the bidding starts out high and then moves lower. Whichever bidder makes the first bid is the winner. The pressure is really on the bidders.

**Variations** We suggested two possible variations for the chocolate auction. The first variation is adding the absolute auction, meaning the highest bidder wins regardless of how low the bid may be. The second variation is adding the reserve bid auction, which means the owner does not have to sell to the highest bidder unless that bid meets or exceeds the owner's reserve bid.

We like the absolute auction variation with the Dutch auction. We have said the risk with an absolute auction is that you must sell to the highest bidder. The reward is that the bidders know this and you may have more bidders interested in bidding. However, with a Dutch auction there is so much pressure on the bidders to bid that we think you will be rewarded (but there are no guarantees).

## *The Auction*

We will assume that you have done all the preparation necessary for your chocolate auction. This is the identical preparation we showed you how to do for the vanilla auction. You have determined that your property is worth $200,000 based on similar properties selling in your area. Everything is the same right up until eight o'clock the evening of your auction. Now the difference between the vanilla auction and the chocolate auction becomes apparent. At eight o'clock in the vanilla auction the auctioneer opens the bidding at $150,000.

**8:00 P.M.** As eight o'clock approaches, Bud will usher the guests to the auction room. When all the guests have been seated with their bidding paddles in hand, the auctioneer will again be introduced by Bud and the auction is set to begin. "Ladies and gentlemen, this is the moment you have all been waiting for. I am going to bring Liam O'Rourke to the front of the room to start the auction."

The auctioneer says, "Ladies and gentlemen, may I have your attention please? Welcome to tonight's auction! My name is Liam O'Rourke. I will be your auctioneer this evening. We are about to begin the auction. Before we do please take a moment to review with me how the auction will be conducted.

This is a Dutch auction with no reserve bid. The winning bidder is the bidder who bids first. This may be a different rule than some of you are familiar with at auctions. I will recognize your bid when you raise your bidding number above your head. The bidding is over when I say so. The bidding results are final.

If you are the winning bidder please see Buck (the money magnate) immediately at the conclusion of the auction. We will open the bidding at $229,000. Every 15 seconds I will lower the bid by $1,000. This will continue until we have a winner. Are there any questions?

**The Bidding**   "$228,000." The buyers have done their homework. "$227,000." They know the market value of your property. "$226,000" As the first few minutes tick away, "$225,000" the price starts to get into the range "$224,000" that some of the buyers have contemplated bidding. "$223,000." The silence is deafening. "$222,000." No one has bid. "$221,000." However, your heart is beating normally. "$220,000." It is the buyers who are starting to experience rapid heartbeat. "$219,000." Each buyer is competing against every other buyer. "$218,000." They are pressured to bid at a price higher than they want to pay. "$217,000." If they wait for the bid to come down, "$216,000," then another buyer, "$215,000," whose motivation they have no clue about, may bid. "$214,000." Remember, the first buyer to bid is the winner! "$213,000." Bidder number 7, Mr. and Mrs. Lucky, are ready to burst. "$212,000."

They can see themselves living in your property. "$211,000." Mrs. Lucky grabs Mr. Lucky's right hand. Up goes bidder number 7's bidder's paddle to signal their bid. "Sold to bidder number 7 for $211,000!"

Congratulations! You have just auctioned your property for top dollar! You have received $11,000 more than the normal full price offer of $200,000! Talk about buyer compression. The Luckys will now meet with Buck, the money magnate, to finalize the sale.

**Confirmation**   You or your auctioneer, will direct the winning bidder to see Buck. He will confirm the winning bid. To do this Buck will reverify the winning bidder's financial information. Buck will then give the winner the details on closing the transaction.

Depending on your state or regional law, you may need to have a formal real estate closing with an attorney or an escrow company. It is possible to have the deed to your home prepared in advance. On the evening of the auction, if the winning bidder has the total amount of the purchase price with him in the form of a cashier's check(s), he could give you the money and you can give him the deed.

# Auction Precautions

We want to conclude this chapter with some auction precautions. Some concern pre-auction considerations; some relate to events during your auction; and some relate to post-auction events. None of these auction precautions are scary or are meant to dissuade you from conducting your auction. We just want to make you aware of them in advance so you are prepared.

## *Auction versus Raffle*

An auction is not a raffle. This is obvious. Some people seem to get this confused from time to time. A raffle is regarded in some locales as a game of chance, gambling if you will. This makes it subject to state or regional law. Unless you are a nonprofit you may be forbidden from holding a raffle. If someone asks you if you are raffling your home your response is, "No, I am auctioning my home."

## *Prevent No-Shows*

One of the ways you can prevent no-shows at your live auction is to diligently follow up with the people who respond to your auction announcement. We recommend you make a reservation for them to attend and then call or e-mail to confirm their attendance the day before the auction. This makes people feel special and taken care of.

When you are talking with people on the phone let them know you are limiting the number of bidders at your auction. You will be happy to reserve them a place if they give you their name and phone number. If people are not willing to do that you know they are not serious about attending your auction.

Make reservations for the first 10 bidders and put people after that on a waiting list. Two days before the auction call the people on your waiting list and confirm they have a reservation whether you discover any bidders dropping out or being noncommittal in your first 10. Remember, you want as many bidders as possible at your auction.

If you have only one bidder show up at your auction then you obviously will not conduct an auction. However, you can always ask that individual to make you an offer. If you have two or three bidders you may make it a spot bid auction with each bidder getting to write down one bid. This will work well if you have a reserve bid for your-self.

### Know Your Bidders

Just as you would like to know something about a buyer who is inter-ested in your property if you are engaged in a conventional sale, you need to take the time to find out about your auction bidders. This knowl-edge can be gained before and during the auction event.

Bud, the bidders' buddy, is the person to take the phone calls from the list of prospective bidders responding to your auction announce-ment. Bud will build rapport with them. By the time they arrive for the auction, Bud will know how motivated they are. The prospective bid-ders will feel they know Bud before they actually meet. During the auc-tion process Bud can brief Buck on each of the bidders.

### Verify Funds

Buck *must* verify bidder funds before giving a guest a bidder's paddle. You cannot allow someone to bid if he is not a legitimate bidder. What if that individual has the winning bid? How will he close the transaction if he has no money? If you have no cash, you cannot attend the bash! If you have no dough, you gotta go!

### Backup Bids

This is your ace in the hole. Usually the winning bidder at your auction has triumphed over one or two bidders who were competing with him right to the end. Have Bud identify those bidders during the auction. As the winning bidder meets with Buck to close the deal, Bud should en-gage the backup bidder in conversation.

Bud will let the backup bidder know that if the winning bidder does not follow through with the closing in a timely manner; the backup bidder could then move into the winning position. Bud is not making the backup bidder any promises, but Bud would like to stay in touch with that individual over the next day or so just in case there is a prob-lem with the winning bidder.

Northbrook Public Library
847-272-6224

03/12/12
01:09 pm

em:The all-new real estate foreclosure,
hort-selling, underwater, property auction,
ositive cash flow book : your ultimate guide
 making money in a crashing market

ue Date: 4/2/2012,23:59

Mon-Thurs 9-9, Fri 9-6
Sat 9-5, Sun 1-5

You have to decide if the original winning bid is the sale price or if you will accept the backup bidder's bid as the sales price. That is up to you. The point is you want to have a backup bidder to replace a winning bidder who does not perform.

## *Buyer's Remorse*

It is possible for the winning bidder to have his auction fever break and come down with buyer's remorse in the time it takes to walk from the auction room to the closing room to meet with Buck.

Our advice is to meet buyer's remorse head on. Buck must ask the winning bidder this question. "Winning Bidder, is there any reason you are aware of that would prevent you from closing?" Buck needs to listen very carefully to the answer. If Buck detects any hedging on the winner's part or feels he will flake out, then Buck must say the following.

"Winning Bidder, the escrow instructions stipulate that barring any agreed upon conditions if you do not complete the closing you will forfeit 10 percent of the purchase price as liquidated damages."

For example, if the purchase price is $211,000 and the Luckys have put $211,000 into escrow, they would forfeit $21,100. If the Luckys put $21,100 into escrow they would forfeit the whole amount. If the Luckys say no problem to this, they will close. If the Luckys balk at this, then Buck may have to ask Bud to bring in your backup bidder.

The good thing about selling your property by auction is the buyer compression that occurs. This tends to make the winning bidder realize that other people think your property is worth it and to feel lucky that he was the one who was able to be the winner. This validates to the winning bidder that he got a good deal.

In the next chapter we will show you a phenomenal new technique. We call it buy low and sell lower. This technique allows you to create cash flow on the financing you create as the seller banker.

# CHAPTER 15

# Buy Low and Sell Lower

In this chapter we are going to show you a phenomenal new technique that you can use as an investor to make money in a crashing real estate market. We expect you are going to become very wealthy using this technique. We refer to this new technique as buy low and sell lower. You are buying for one price and selling for a lower price. You are taking advantage of the price decline environment in the crashing real estate market.

This is not about hoping you are buying at the bottom of the market just before it turns around and goes back up. Although that would be great, the bottom of the real estate market is not yet in sight. As far as when the turnaround in the real estate market will happen, later rather than sooner is going to be the case.

## Buy Low and Sell High

Buy low and sell high is the number one real estate, stock, bond, mutual fund, and any other financial investment strategy. Buy low and sell high is still a great real estate investment strategy. Of course, as we have already said, the problem in a crashing real estate market is how do you do that?

It is still possible in a crashing market to buy low and sell high if you find a fluke situation. We checked on a property in a very nice neighborhood that was on the market at an unbelievably low price. It was listed for $99,900. It was worth $150,000 just as it sat even though it needed work. There was $50,000 on the table.

### On the Table

| | |
|---|---|
| Market value | $150,000 |
| Listed for | −99,900 |
| On the table | $ 50,100 |

The real estate agent along with the circumstances combined to create this fluke situation. The owner was on an extended stay in the Gray Bar motel. The real estate agent was working with the owner's mother to sell the property quickly to raise cash. Neither the agent nor the mother had any idea of what the property was worth. Just a side note here: not all agents know what they are doing so it is critical that when you work with an agent you find one who has a proven track record of knowledge and a good reputation.

## Bidding War

We wound up in a bidding war with three other investors. We were all making cash offers. We wound up getting the property for $127,000. The agent later admitted to us that she had probably priced the property too low.

We turned around and sold the property within five days for $143,000 to another investor with expertise in rehabbing. We made a quick $16,000. So in a crashing real estate market we had used the buy low and sell high strategy.

### Our Profit

| | |
|---|---|
| Sold | $143,000 |
| Paid | −127,000 |
| Our profit | $ 16,000 |

## Buy Low and Sell Lower

What is more realistic is to figure out a strategy to use when real estate prices are continuing in a downward spiral. The strategy to consistently make money in a crashing market must revolve around the terms of the deal. The terms you buy for and the terms you sell for are where you can make money.

We learned very early in our real estate investing that price and terms were the two keys to making any real estate deal work. The way to make money when you buy low and sell lower is on the terms. Following is how this can be done.

## Make Money on the Terms

We bought a property at a short-sale for $225,000. We had valued the property at $252,000. It looked like we had a $27,000 profit coming our way. We felt we had made a win going in deal.

### Win Going in

| | |
|---|---|
| Property value | $252,000 |
| Short-sale price | −225,000 |
| Win going in | $ 27,000 |

Then the real estate market crashed. The market dropped 20 percent seemingly overnight.

### 20% Market Drop

| | |
|---|---|
| Property value | $252,000 |
| Market drop | × 20% |
| 20% market drop | $ 50,400 |

Instead of the property being valued at $252,000, it was now worth closer to $200,000.

### Crashed Market Value

| | |
|---|---|
| Property value | $252,000 |
| 20% market drop | −50,400 |
| Crashed market value | $201,600 |

Lucky for us we had gotten a wholesale price at the short-sale. Otherwise we would have been looking at a potential $50,000 loss. As it was, we were still looking at a potential $25,000 loss.

### Potential Loss

| | |
|---|---|
| Short-sale price | $225,000 |
| Crashed market value | 201,600 |
| Potential loss | $ 23,400 |

We were not going to be able to sell the property for $225,000 let alone $252,000. We wanted to cover our potential $25,000 loss plus make money on the deal. What was the best way out of our dilemma?

## The Deal

We owned the property free and clear. We sold the property for $200,000. We got a $25,000 cash down payment from the buyer. The buyer was not able to qualify for any bank financing because of some credit dings. We agreed to be the seller banker for the balance of the purchase price of $175,000.

### The Deal

| | |
|---|---|
| Purchase price | $200,000 |
| Down payment | −25,000 |
| Seller banker | $175,000 |

We now had $25,000 cash back in hand on our $225,000 cash short-sale deal. Instead of carrying just a first mortgage of $175,000, we carried a first mortgage of $50,000, a second mortgage of $50,000, and a third mortgage of $75,000 for a total of $175,000.

### Seller Banker

| | |
|---|---|
| First mortgage | $ 50,000 |
| Second mortgage | 50,000 |
| Third mortgage | +75,000 |
| Total mortgages | $175,000 |

### *The Mortgages*

We told the property buyer that we would give him a 10 percent annual interest rate on the overall $175,000 we were carrying for him as the seller banker. This would make his annual interest payment $17,500.

There would be a balloon payment after five years of the $175,000 principal.

### Annual Interest Payment

| | |
|---|---|
| Mortgage amount | $175,000 |
| Annual interest rate | × 10% |
| Annual interest payment | $ 17,500 |

The interest-only payment would be payable monthly at $1,458.33.

### Monthly Interest Payment

$$\frac{\$17,500}{\$12 \text{ MONTHS}} = \$1,458.33 \text{ MONTHLY}$$

As we said, we divided up the $175,000 into a first, second, and third mortgage. The first mortgage of $50,000 was payable interest-only monthly at 11 percent annual interest. The second mortgage of $50,000 was payable interest-only monthly at 15 percent annual interest. The third mortgage of $75,000 was payable interest-only monthly at 6 percent annual interest.

### Seller Banker

| | |
|---|---|
| First mortgage | $ 50,000 @ 11% |
| Second mortgage | $ 50,000 @ 15% |
| Third mortgage | +$ 75,000 @ 6% |
| Total mortgages | $175,000 @ 10% |

Let's look at the numbers a little more closely. The annual interest the buyer is paying on the $175,000 we said is $17,500. The annual interest on the first, second, and third mortgages also has to be $17,500. Do the calculations. . . .

| | | |
|---|---|---|
| First $50,000 @ 11% | = | $ 5,500 annually |
| Second $50,000 @ 15% | = | $ 7,500 annually |
| Third $75,000 @ 6% | = | $ 4,500 annually |
| Total | | $17,500 annually |

. . . Voila! The annual interest amounts match.

## Make Money

Now we had the flexibility we needed to make some money. We took the first mortgage of $50,000 and traded it for a $75,000 parcel of land.

We took the second mortgage of $50,000 and sold it for $60,000 to another investor who wanted income. We took the third mortgage of $75,000 and sold the $375 monthly cash flow to an investor for $15,000. Take a look at how this played out.

### First Mortgage of $50,000

We traded the first mortgage of $50,000 for a parcel of land worth $75,000. We explained to the land owner that he would receive $77,500 in principal and interest by holding the mortgage for five years.

**Five-Year Value of First Mortgage of $50,000**

First mortgage of $50,000 @ 11%  =

$ 5,500 interest
× 5 years
$27,500 interest
+ $50,000 principal payoff
$77,500 value of first mortgage

We then immediately sold the parcel of land for $75,000 with no money down. We were the seller banker and carried a first mortgage for the entire purchase price of $75,000 at 10 percent annual interest. The annual interest was $7,500.

**Five-Year Value of First Mortgage of $75,000**

First mortgage of $75,000 @ 10%  =

$ 7,500 interest
× 5 years
$ 37,500 interest
+ $ 75,000 principal payoff
$112,500 value of first mortgage

We picked up $25,000 in equity by trading the first mortgage of $50,000 for the $75,000 parcel of land. We replaced the cash flow of $5,500 in annual interest on the first mortgage of $50,000 with the cash flow of $7,500 in annual interest on the first mortgage of $75,000. Over five years this generated an additional $10,000 for us.

**Additional Funds to US**

First $75,000 @ 10%  =          $ 7,500 interest annually
First $50,000 @ 11%  =          −5,500 interest annually
                                $ 2,000 interest annually
                                × 5 years
Additional funds $10,000 to us

Essentially by upgrading from the first mortgage of $50,000 to the first mortgage of $75,000 we profited $35,000.

### Upgrade Profit

| | |
|---|---|
| Equity profit | $25,000 |
| Interest profit | +10,000 |
| Total profit | $35,000 |

## Second Mortgage of $50,000

We said we sold the second mortgage of $50,000 to another investor who wanted income. Why would this other investor pay us $60,000 cash, which was $10,000 more than the face amount of the second mortgage?

Remember we had attached an annual interest rate of 15 percent on this second mortgage. The investor was willing to pay us a $10,000 premium to be able to benefit from this high rate of return.

## Investor Return

Let's see how the investor made out. The investor was paying us $60,000. He would be receiving $7,500 annual interest on the second mortgage of $50,000. He would receive this annual interest for five years. After five years he would receive a $50,000 balloon payment.

### Five-Year Value of Second Mortgage

Second $50,000 @ 15%  =  $ 7,500 interest
$\times$ 5 years
$37,500 interest
+  50,000 principal payoff
$87,500 value of second mortgage

The investor paid us $60,000 for this $87,500 investment return over five years. This means the investor received his $60,000 original investment back plus an additional $27,500 profit.

### Investor Profit

| | |
|---|---|
| Investment return | $87,500 |
| Amount invested | −60,000 |
| Investor profit | $27,500 |

The investor received almost a 46 percent total return on his five-year investment.

**Five-Year Total Return**

$$\frac{\$27,500}{\$60,000} = 45.83\% \text{ total return}$$

This translates into the investor receiving over 9 percent as an annual return on his investment.

**Annual Return**

45.83% total return / 5 years   =   9.17% annual return

So how did we make out on our second mortgage? We turned a $50,000 mortgage note into $60,000 in cash.

### Third Mortgage of $75,000

As we said we took the third mortgage of $75,000 and sold the $375 monthly cash flow to an investor for $15,000 cash. We retained the rights to the $75,000 principal payment due in five years.

## How Did We Do?

Follow us through this as we show you the benefit of buy low and sell lower. We originally invested $225,000 in cash in a short-sale property. The market crashed and we could only sell the property for $200,000. We were trying to figure out how to make our $25,000 back. We also wanted to replace the $27,000 we lost from what we had determined was the $252,000 property value and our $225,000 short-sale price.

### Cash Received

Let's see how we came out. We will start with the cash. We received $25,000 in cash as a down payment when we sold our short-sale property  We received $60,000 in cash when we sold our second mortgage of $50,000. We received $15,000 in cash when we sold the cash flow from our third mortgage of $75,000. This is a total of $100,000 in cash.

#### Cash Received

| | |
|---|---:|
| Down payment | $ 25,000 |
| Sale of second mortgage | 60,000 |
| Sale of third mortgage cash flow | +15,000 |
| Cash received | $100,000 |

### *Mortgages Payoffs*

Next we will look at the mortgage payoffs. We turned the first mortgage of $50,000 into a first mortgage of $75,000 when we bought and sold the parcel of land. We carried a third mortgage of $75,000 when we sold our short-sale property. This is a total of $150,000 in mortgage payoffs.

#### Mortgage Payoffs

| | |
|---|---:|
| First mortgage of | $ 75,000 |
| Third mortgage of | + 75,000 |
| Mortgage payoffs | $150,000 |

### *Interest Received*

And finally we will include the interest we received. We received $7,500 yearly for five years on the first mortgage of $75,000 we carried on the sale of the parcel of land. This is a total of $37,500 in interest received.

#### Interest Received

First mortgage of $75,000 @ 10%  =  $ 7,500 interest
$\times$ 5 years
$37,500 interest

## Total Received

We received $100,000 in cash. We received $150,000 in mortgage payoffs. We received $37,500 in interest. We received a total of $287,500.

### Total Received

| | |
|---|---|
| Cash | $100,000 |
| Mortgages | 150,000 |
| Interest | + 37,500 |
| Total | $287,500 |

We think we did alright. What do you think? By taking the time to think outside the box regarding our price to sell we were inspired to look at our terms and create ways where we and everyone involved with us could win through terms! We bought low and sold lower and still made money in what most everyone else would have said was an impossible situation. In the next chapter we will talk about our strategy of cash and cash flow.

# CHAPTER 16

# Cash and Cash Flow Is King

Cash and cash flow is king in a crashing real estate market. The old adage is you have to spend money to make money. The problem is you have to have money to spend. What if you have little or no money to get started investing in real estate? In other words, what if you have a cash and cash flow problem?

Almost 30 years ago, Robert Allen proved in *Nothing Down* that you could get started as a successful real estate investor without cash and cash flow. He said publicly that he could be sent to any city in the United States, be given just $100 in spending money, and within three days he would be able to buy real estate using none of his own money or credit.

The *Los Angeles Times* took him up on his bold statement. It had a reporter accompany Bob to a city chosen by the newspaper: San Francisco. They got off the plane, the reporter gave Bob five $20 bills, and the clock started.

Fifty-six hours later Bob Allen had signed contracts on six properties totaling $750,000. He did this using none of his own money or credit. After the newspaper published this story a new possibility dawned for the small real estate investor with no cash or cash flow to become successful investing in real estate.

## Cash and Cash Flow without Owning Real Estate

Now is your time to be bold. This chapter is about being bold in creating cash and cash flow in your real estate investing. We have already shared with you in this book many ways to create cash and cash flow. Remember the seller banker conversation?

Short selling is a great way to make cash and cash flow. However, it requires that you have cash or access to cash like a money partner from the outset. Unfortunately a short-selling lender is not going to accept your nothing-down deal. And you have to own the property before you can make cash and cash flow.

We are going to share with you another way to make cash and cash flow investing in real estate without owning real estate. The owning of the real estate is what brings the cash intensive aspect into play. If you do not have to actually own the real estate, your lack of cash or cash flow will not hinder you from immediately investing in this crashing real estate market.

## Assigning Real Estate Contracts

One way we make cash and cash flow is through assigning real estate contracts, deal after deal. Time and time again! (Remember the real estate deal business from earlier?) Assigning real estate contracts is a way to flip real estate without buying or owning the property. You may not even have to close escrow.

We are actually flipping real estate contracts. Real estate contracts are personal property. We own the contracts. Once you know how to assign contracts, your ability to make cash and cash flow happen is going to take off.

## What Is Assigning?

Assigning a real estate contract transfers your position in the contract to another person for an agreed fee. Said technically, assigning a real estate contract allows you, the assignor, to assign the contract to a new person, the assignee. An assignment transfers your rights to purchase a property under the terms of a real estate purchase contract to a new buyer.

The new buyer steps into your shoes and can buy the property under the same terms and conditions you negotiated with the seller. So if you have negotiated a really good deal you can make cash and cash flow without buying and owning the property. The assignor (you) assigns your contract to the assignee (buyer) in return for an assignment fee.

**Assignment**

Assignment →

Assignor          Assignee
You          Buyer

← Cash

## Assignment Fees

The cash and cash flow you receive for assigning a contract is called an assignment fee. This fee is negotiable between you, the assignor, and the person you assign the contract to, the assignee.

The other party to the contract you have had accepted—seller, optionor, lender, lessor, or whomever—has no say in your negotiations with your assignee. (However, as mentioned earlier, some short-selling lenders may balk at your doing an assignment of your short-selling contract.)

What size should the fee be that you receive for assigning a contract? We have assigned a contract for as little as $1,000. We have also assigned a contract for as much as $100,000. Typically, fees received for assigning contracts range between $5,000 and $15,000, perhaps more if it is a phenomenal deal. That is to be determined between you and the assignee.

## How to Assign a Contract

Assigning a contract begins when you write the initial offer. In the initial offer you make to the property owner, whether it is a purchase contract, an option contract, a mortgage contract, or a trust deed, you use the terminology "and/or assigns" in the contract.

## Assignment Contract

Earlier in the book we showed you how to assign a real estate contract using the and/or assigns name addition. What about an actual assignment contract? We find that having an assignment contract available makes assigning any contract a more viable option.

You still want and/or assigns in the buyer's name section in whatever contract you are writing. By using the assignment contract in conjunction with and/or assigns, you build an added layer of written protection for yourself as the assignor and for the assignee.

## Why Use an Assignment?

There are four main reasons for using an assignment. Assigning a purchase contract is the first way to make cash and cash flow without owning the property. Assigning is the fastest way to flip a property. Assigning is the quickest way to make money in real estate investing. Assigning avoids all the potential pitfalls of real estate ownership that you could find yourself involved with if you did not do an assignment.

## Assigning Makes You Money without Owning Property

Assigning a real estate contract makes you money without owning property. In a traditional real estate investment, you (the investor) make cash and cash flow by finding a property, writing and having your offer accepted by the seller, opening and successfully closing an escrow, fixing up the property (if necessary), and then selling the property to a buyer. This is what a timeline would look like for buying and owning real estate to make money:

### Timeline for Buying and Owning Real Estate to Make Money

| Find Property | Write Offer | Offer Accepted | Open Escrow | Close Escrow | Fix up | Sell Property |
|---|---|---|---|---|---|---|
| | | | | Spend Money | Spend Money | Make Money |

We are being rather generous with the timeline. It is actually harder than that. The reality of making cash and cash flow when you buy real estate the traditional way begins with that timeline. You really don't make any money until you do the following: advertise and show the property, receive and accept an offer, and open and close an escrow. Then, and only then, do you make money.

### Selling Timeline for Owning Real Estate to Make Money

| Advertise Property | Show Property | Receive Offer | Accept Offer | Open Escrow | Close Escrow |
| --- | --- | --- | --- | --- | --- |

Spend Money                                                              Make Money

## Assigning Is the Fastest Way to Flip Property

Assigning a real estate contract is the fastest way to flip property. Let's face it. Paperwork is the name of the game in real estate investing. The less paperwork involved in a real estate transaction, the better.

Less paperwork involved in a real estate transaction means less time to complete the transaction.

The less time you and the real estate investor or retail buyer you are assigning the contract to must invest in the transaction means a faster turnaround time for you to generate cash and cash flow.

### *Paperwork for Flip without Escrow*

This is the paperwork involved in the simplest flip we do: buying the property and then selling the property. There is no escrow involved. We write a purchase contract and an earnest money promissory note for a nothing down deal. We present this paperwork to the property owners.

They accept our offer. They give us back our promissory note and a quitclaim deed to transfer title to the property. This involves three distinct pieces of paperwork for the buying side.

### For Buying Property

1. Real estate purchase contract
2. Promissory note
3. Quitclaim deed

We receive a purchase contract and a personal check as an earnest money deposit from an investor we flip the property to. We give the real estate investor a quitclaim deed.

The investor gives us a cashier's check. We give the investor back his personal check. Again, we don't have an escrow between the investor and us. We have an additional four distinct pieces of paperwork on the selling side.

### For Selling Side

1. Real estate purchase contract
2. Personal check
3. Quitclaim deed
4. Cashier's check

Now we have a total of seven distinct pieces of paperwork involved in this transaction. There are three pieces of paperwork on the buying side. There are four pieces of paper on the selling side.

## Paperwork for Assignment

What if we were able to have just assigned our purchase contract instead of doing a traditional flip where we actually owned something? Would we speed up the flip by doing an assignment? How much paperwork is involved if we assign our purchase contract?

We write a purchase contract and a promissory note, which we present to the property owner. The owner gives us back our promissory note. So far, everything is the same as doing a flip.

Here is where the assignment transaction changes the paperwork. The property owner does not give us a quitclaim deed. He gives a quitclaim deed to transfer title to the investor to whom we assign the purchase contract. We now have one less quitclaim deed using the assignment.

The next change in paperwork with the assignment is the lack of a second purchase contract. We do not receive a purchase contract from the investor. The investor takes over our position in the first purchase contract.

The investor does not write a personal check to accompany his offer to us. We receive a cashier's check from the investor for our assignment fee. The investor receives the quitclaim deed from the property owner.

**Assignment Paperwork**

1. Real estate purchase contract
2. Promissory note
3. Quitclaim deed
4. Cashier's check

The difference in the amount of paperwork for a flip and an assignment is substantial. The flip paperwork runs to seven items. The assignment paperwork runs to four items. What happens after we assign the contract and get paid is between the seller and the assignee/buyer.

## Assigning Is the Quickest Way to Make Cash and Cash Flow

Assigning a real estate contract is the fastest way to make cash and cash flow in real estate investing. When you are using a quick cash strategy, time is definitely of the essence.

The timeline for assigning contracts is substantially shorter than the timeline for a traditional real estate investment. Even when flipping a property, you can't make money as quickly as when you assign contracts.

As you can see, you can make money quicker and at more junctures along the way than with a traditional real estate investment strategy of buy the property, own the property, and sell the property.

**Assigning Contracts to Make Money**

| Find Property | Write Offer | Offer Accepted | Open Escrow | Close Escrow | Fix up | Sell Property |
|---|---|---|---|---|---|---|
| | | Make Money | Make Money | Make Money | | |

## Assigning Avoids the Pitfalls of Real Estate Ownership

Assigning a contract avoids all the potential pitfalls of real estate ownership. Assigning property contracts has multiple advantages over the traditional buy-and-hold property investment strategy.

These advantages include no rehabbing, no acting as a landlord, no monthly mortgage payments, no property taxes, no hazard insurance, no maintenance costs, no homeowner's association dues, no lawsuits, no extensive record keeping, and no income tax problems.

## When to Assign a Contract

You can assign a real estate contract before, during, and after the closing of the escrow. Assigning a contract before the closing is the way we like to do our property transactions. You tie up a property with an accepted contract and immediately search for a buyer to whom to assign the contract.

Assigning a contract during the escrow period/closing is our second favorite way to do our transactions. You tie up the property and assign the contract before the closing takes place. The assignee takes your place in the escrow and then winds up closing on the escrow.

Assigning after the closing is the final way we like to do our transactions. Again, you tie up a property with an assignment clause in the contract. If you don't find a buyer before closing and wind up closing on the property yourself, you can quickly transfer your interest in the property to another buyer after that closing. Essentially, you are going to flip the property using what we call an assignment deed.

Look at the timeline for assigning contracts. This will give you a way to visualize the different times you can use an assignment. Anytime you can assign a contract and make cash and cash flow is a good time to do an assignment.

To reiterate, you can assign your contract after you have an accepted offer and before an escrow is opened. You can assign your contract during the escrow period. And, you can assign your contract after closing escrow.

### Timeline for Assigning Contracts

| Accepted Offer | Open Escrow | Close Escrow |
|---|---|---|
| Assign | Assign | Assign |
| Before | During | After |
| Closing | Closing | Closing |

Once you assimilate the assigning tactic into your investing strategy, you will begin to find all kinds of contracts to assign. Contracts to assign will begin to find you. We look to assign most every contract we write. Let's talk about another tool to use for making cash and cash flow work for you. That tool is option contracts.

## Option Contracts

A real estate option contract gives you the right to buy a property without the obligation to buy the property. With a normal purchase contract, when the buyer and seller have a meeting of the minds and sign it, the buyer must perform and go through with the agreed-on purchase. If the buyer does not perform based on the terms of the contract, the seller can sue the buyer for specific performance.

An option contract allows the buyer and seller to have a meeting of the minds and sign the option contract, while offering the buyer a specified period of time to exercise the option. If the buyer does not exercise the option, the option expires, and the buyer owes no further obligation to the seller.

Put another way, an option contract gives a potential buyer the right to purchase a property before the specified future date in the contract for the amount and under the terms and conditions written in the contract.

## Optionor/Optionee

In an option contract, the parties to the contract are the optionor and the optionee. The optionor provides real estate paperwork, the option contract, to the optionee. In return, the optionee gives money to the optionor for granting the option. This is called the option fee. The seller is the optionor. The buyer is the optionee.

**Option**

Option →

Optionor                    Optionee
Seller                      Buyer

← Cash

## Option Fee

The cash and cash flow you receive for giving an option is called an option fee. The option fee is the consideration given by the optionee to the optionor. This is what satisfies the consideration requirement and makes an option contract valid. As we have said, in return for the option fee, the optionor gives the option to the optionee to purchase the property.

The option fee is usually a percentage of the agreed-on purchase price for the property. This percentage can range from as low as 0.5 percent on a higher priced property to as much as 10 percent on a lower priced property. For a $100 million purchase price, the option fee may be $500,000. On a $300,000 purchase price the option fee may be $30,000.

### Option Fee Percentages

| $100,000,000 | Purchase price | $300,000 |
|---|---|---|
| × 0.5% | Option percent | × 10% |
| $ 500,000 | Option fee | $ 30,000 |

The option fee can be applied to the purchase price in the event the optionee exercises the option to purchase. Sometimes the option fee does not apply to the purchase price. This may happen when a second or third option time period is negotiated. We always negotiate the option fee applying to the purchase price regardless. That way, if we exercise the option, we already have money credited to the deal.

Options are used for many reasons: leverage, conservation of funds, leaving a way out, protecting a possibility, privacy, and so forth. There are many reasons to use an option. Check out the following story.

## Walt Disney

Walt Disney assembled the property for Walt Disney World in Florida using option contracts. He did not want to tip his hand to the many different property owners from whom he needed to purchase property. If remaining property owners knew he was buying property, they could hold out for a higher price. Disney would have had to pay big bucks once word got out that he wanted to put all the properties together for Walt Disney World.

## Option Advantage

The advantages of controlling property with an option contract are the same as the advantages of controlling property with an assignment contract. You can flip the option contract rather than flipping the property. In other words, with an option contract you control the property without owning it.

We use an option contract when we need to assemble partners to go in on a real estate transaction. Sometimes these partners are money partners. Sometimes they are developers. Sometimes they are home builders.

## How to Option

Optioning begins with the option contract. You can take a standard purchase contract and turn it into an option contract. Or you can use an option contract from the beginning of the transaction.

A real estate option contract is similar to a grant deed or warranty deed in that only the seller needs to sign the document to make it valid. Just as in a grant deed or warranty deed, the seller will be granting something in an option contract.

In a grant deed or warranty deed, the seller is granting title or ownership in the property to the buyer. In an option contract the seller grants the right for the buyer to buy the property during the option period for a price agreed on in the contract.

## Purchase Contracts

You can start with a purchase contract and turn it into an option contract. To do this, go to the supplements section of the contract. This is the section in the purchase contract that says that the attached documents are incorporated into the purchase contract. Add the real estate option contract to this section. Attach the option contract to the purchase contract. The two contracts together become one contract when the option is exercised.

## Option Contracts

We recommend using an option contract from the beginning of the transaction. That way, both you and the property owner know you are interested in putting together an option at the outset of negotiations.

### *Memorandum of Option*

A memorandum of option can be recorded to protect your optionee interest in the property. Your name as the optionee does not have to appear on the memorandum of option. If the optionor, or property owner, does try to sell the property to another buyer during your option period a title company, while doing a title search for the other buyer, will uncover the recorded memorandum of option. This will prevent the property owner from transferring clear title, and the deal with the other buyer will fall apart.

### *Assigning an Option Contract*

We use an option contract that is already set up to be assigned by the wording in the contract itself. In the event you are using an option contract that is not set up to be assigned, all you have to do is add the words "and/or assigns" to the buyer's name portion of the contract.

By assigning your option contract you make cash and cash flow immediately. You do not have to put up the option fee. You, as the optionee, assign your option contact to your assignee. Your assignee is then responsible for putting up the option fee.

| **Option Contract** | | **Assign Option Contract** | |
| --- | --- | --- | --- |
| | Option → | | Assign → |
| Optionor seller | Optionee buyer/You | Assignor You | Assignee Optionee |
| | ← Cash | | ← Cash |

### *Cash and Cash Flow System*

If you remember back to what you learned earlier in this book about being the seller banker and being in the real estate deal business, you can see that the combination of these concepts and the use of an assignment/option technique make for one powerful cash and cash flow system.

You find a deal, make it, restructure it with a spread from the wholesale price you get it for to a fair retail price for a buyer with you acting as the seller banker. Then you assign an option to it for a fee (cash). When the option is exercised you collect the cash for the balance of the down payment and cash flow from the monthly payments. Voila! A successful cash and cash flow system!

In the next chapter we will give you our take on the future of the real estate market. The future of the global real estate market has already been assured by the governments of the world. There will be coordinated governmental moves that will bail out the global real estate market. That gives us as real estate investors a huge opportunity to make cash and cash flow.

# CHAPTER 17

# The Future of the Real Estate Market

The future of the global real estate market has already been assured by the governments of the world. The global real estate market is being bailed out. The mortgage market and the real estate market in the United States are ground zero for the worldwide economic collapse. To fix the global economy, the real estate market in the United States must be revived from its moribund state.

The good news is that the real estate market in the United States is being revived. The bad news is the patient may not survive the economic medicine being administered to bring about the real estate market's resuscitation.

As a real estate investor you need to pay close attention to this economic medicine. It will have a direct impact on the success of your real estate investments. To better understand what we will share with you in this chapter we want to first talk about something most everyone has heard about to some extent in their lifetime.

## CPR

In the old paradigm in medicine when a person had a heart attack and his heart stopped two things were done. A type of CPR was performed that called for chest compressions to restart the heart and oxygen was blown into the victim's mouth (mouth-to-mouth resuscitation).

The paramedics would continue CPR and administer oxygen as they transported the patient to the hospital. Once at the hospital, doctors worked feverishly to rapidly restart the heart and continue to administer large amounts of pure oxygen to the patient. After 20 to 30 minutes if the patient wasn't revived, he was pronounced dead. So why did the CPR not work?

Research has shown that what kills cells is the rapid reperfusion of oxygen. So what kills the heart muscle after it has stopped beating and been deprived of oxygen is the rapid reintroduction of massive amounts of oxygen as it is shocked into beating again.

## New Paradigm

We now know that when cells are deprived of oxygen, even for many minutes, they are still alive. There is enough latent oxygen in the human body to keep the cells alive for an extended period of time.

Just think of the news stories of people who have been resuscitated after falling through the ice and being underwater for 20 or 30 minutes.

In the new paradigm in medicine, when a person has a heart attack and the heart stops, a different type of CPR is now performed. The emphasis is on chest compressions to restart the heart. Little or no blowing of oxygen into the victim's mouth is required.

Once at the hospital if the patient's heart is still not beating he is put on a heart-lung bypass machine. The patient's body temperature is lowered through therapeutic hypothermia. Oxygen is slowly introduced back into the patient's body. Then the patient's heart is restarted. This new technique seems to allow for greater long-term survival rates. Now let's go back to our real estate investing conversation.

## Inflation: The Oxygen of the Global Economy

Inflation is the oxygen of the global economy. With no inflation for a prolonged period of time, the global economy dies. The global economy has suffered a potentially fatal attack. Deflation is killing the patient. In order to resuscitate the global economy inflation must be reintroduced. How much and when it is reintroduced will be critical to the long-term survival of the global economy.

# What Is Inflation?

A good working definition for inflation is this: Inflation occurs when too many dollars chase too few goods and services. Inflation means the same goods and services will cost more money in the future than they cost today. Another way to say this is that in the future money will be worth less than it is today.

## *Rule of 72*

Remember the Rule of 72 from earlier? The Rule of 72 can help us here. We can determine the loss in purchasing power of the dollar by using the Rule of 72 with inflation. Dividing 72 by the annual inflation rate tells us how many years it will be before our purchasing power is cut in half.

### Inflation and Purchasing Power

1% annual inflation, in 72 years our purchasing power is cut in half.
2% annual inflation, in 36 years our purchasing power is cut in half.
3% annual inflation, in 24 years our purchasing power is cut in half.
4% annual inflation, in 18 years our purchasing power is cut in half.
6% annual inflation, in 12 years our purchasing power is cut in half.
8% annual inflation, in 9 years our purchasing power is cut in half.
12% annual inflation, in 6 years our purchasing power is cut in half.
18% annual inflation, in 4 years our purchasing power is cut in half.

## *Actual Annual Inflation Rates*

If you are thinking that the 6 percent, 8 percent, 12 percent, and 18 percent annual inflation rates are theoretical, then think again. Let's look at the actual annual inflation rates from 1976 through 1982 in the United States.

### Actual Annual Inflation Rates in the United States
### 1976–1982

1976 Annual Inflation Rate 6%
1977 Annual Inflation Rate 7%
1978 Annual Inflation Rate 8%
1979 Annual Inflation Rate 13%
1980 Annual Inflation Rate 18%
1981 Annual Inflation Rate 12%
1982 Annual Inflation Rate 9%

## *Bill's Inflated House*

So what do inflation rates and inflation have to do with real estate prices? Inflation rates have a direct impact on real estate prices. Bill bought his first house in Cardiff, California, in 1976 for $43,000. Bill sold this house in 1979 for $80,000. This was an 86 percent price increase.

The house was three years older in 1979 than in 1976. Bill had not done any upgrading or improvements to the house. Was the 1979 house really worth 86 percent more than the 1976 house? The answer is yes and no.

First think about the value of the money. The 1979 house was worth 80,000 1979 dollars. The 1979 house was not worth 80,000 1976 dollars. Money in 1979 was worth less than money in 1976. The real estate purchasing power of the 1979 money was worth less than the real estate purchasing power of the 1976 money.

## *Compounding*

The 6 percent, 7 percent, 8 percent, and 13 percent inflation rates respectively for 1976 through 1979 were compounding from one year to the next. Even compounding does not explain the 86 percent price increase on Bill's house.

### Compounding on Bill's Inflated House

1976 at 6% $43,000 to $45,600
1977 at 7% $45,600 to $48,800
1978 at 8% $48,800 to $52,700
1979 at 13% $52,700 to $59,500

The compounding inflation rate price of Bill's house was $59,500! The difference between the actual 1979 sales price of $80,000 and the compounding price of $59,500 is $20,500.

### Difference Between Actual and Compounding Price

| | |
|---|---|
| Actual price | $ 80,000 |
| Compounding price | −59,500 |
| Difference | $ 20,500 |

Why is there such a difference? What caused this to happen?

### *Market Expectation*

The real estate market's expectation of future inflation drove real estate prices upward beyond the actual inflation rates. The $20,500 difference between the actual price and the compounding price was 34 percent!

### % Difference Between Actual and Compounding Price

$$\frac{\$20,500}{\$59,500} \ = \ 34\%$$

In other words the $80,000 actual price was another 34 percent higher than the $59,500 compounding inflation rate price.

## Protect Yourself from Inflation

The economy doctors have prescribed inflation for the global economy. Inflation is being reintroduced into the global economy. It looks like the patient may recover. God bless inflation!

Hopefully, the doctors attending to the global economy's recovery will be carefully monitoring how much more inflation is necessary and when enough is enough to avoid too much reperfusion of inflation into the global economy.

### *Due Diligence*

Let's do our due diligence with the attending global economy doctors. What is the amount of money the United States government is going to be pumping into the global economy over the next four years? We said earlier, that according to published reports, the figure is $9.7 trillion.

Does anyone believe that this figure will stay this low? A more realistic figure is $13 trillion to $17 trillion of United States central bank (read Federal Reserve) money creation.

The questions we as real estate investors have to answer are the following: What will this do to the inflation rates for 2009, 2010, 2011, 2012, and 2013? How will this affect the global economy? How will this affect the United States and global real estate markets?

### *100-Year Anniversary*

In 2013, the United States Federal Reserve will mark its 100th anniversary. In the early 1980s the number one job of the Fed was to harness inflation. As you can see from the inflation rates from 1976 through 1982, inflation peaked in 1980 and began to decline from there.

### *Attack the Real Estate Market*

The Federal Reserve was able to harness inflation by attacking the real estate market in the United States. They did this by raising interest rates to 17 percent for real estate loans. This effectively cut the demand for real estate and stopped the real estate market in its tracks.

Very few buyers could qualify for real estate loans. Those buyers that could qualify were not interested in paying usurious interest rates and stayed out of the residential real estate market. Inflation began to abate.

Of course, the Fed's actions threw the United States and the global economy into a recession. Retail and wholesale buyers were now operating in a crashed real estate market. There simply was no credit available for buyers to buy real estate. Does this sound familiar?

### *Seller Bankers*

The only real estate that was selling back then was financed by the owner, a role we have dubbed seller banker. Essentially, we as real estate investors have the Federal Reserve to thank for forcing us to invent creative financing in order to survive. For those of you who helped usher in the creative financing revolution back then, we salute you.

## *Ironic Twist*

Paul Volcker was the chairman of the Federal Reserve Bank appointed by President Carter in 1979 who led the Fed in crushing the United States real estate market. In an ironic twist, Mr. Volcker was appointed chairman of a special economic advisory panel by then-President-Elect Obama in November 2008!

The doctor of deflation is now an advising specialist to the doctors of inflation attempting to resuscitate the global economy. We said earlier that how much inflation and when it is reintroduced will be critical to the long-term survival of the global economy. Doctor Volcker; please do not allow them to infuse the patient with too much inflation too quickly.

## *The Bottom Line*

Since 1913, when the Federal Reserve banking system was created in the United States, the inflation rate in the United States is 1,929 percent. That means that a property that cost $10,000 in 1913 costs $192,900 in 2009. We like that kind of appreciation.

### Appreciation

| | |
|---|---|
| 2009 property cost | $192,900 |
| 1913 property cost | −10,000 |
| Appreciation | $182,900 |

However, said another way, in less than 100 years, money has been devalued in the United States by over 1,900 percent.

Being conservative, we think that the inflation rate from 1913 to 2013 will easily exceed 2,000 percent. So that property that cost $10,000 in 1913 will cost at least $200,000 in 2013. Brain trust hint: We think that same property in 2013 will cost at least $300,000.

## *100-Year Plans*

We are big advocates of 100-year plans. The problem most people who are alive today are going to have is not dying too young but rather living too long. People are going to outlive their money unless they prepare now to do something about it.

Over the next 100 years, we think the inflation rate will be 10 times the inflation rate of the last 100 years or 20,000 percent.

**Inflation Rate Next 100 Years**

| | |
|---|---|
| Last 100 years | 2,000% |
| Increased by 10 | × 10 |
| Next 100 years | 20,000% |

That means that a property that cost 200,000 in 2013 will cost $40,000,000 in 2113!

**2113 Cost**

| | |
|---|---|
| 2013 cost | $  200,000 |
| Inflation % | × 20,000% |
| 2113 cost | $40,000,000 |

### Buy Real Estate

The best investment to make to protect yourself and your family from the possible economically lethal affects of the coming hyperinflation is to buy real estate. And we recommend you buy real estate with the intent of holding it for long-term wealth building.

In a period of hyperinflation real estate is king. The longer you hold onto your cash when inflation is running rampant, the less purchasing power you have. Buying and holding assets like real estate that go up in value during periods of hyperinflation is where the smart money is headed.

## Conclusion

The global economy cycles through four phases. The cycle is one of expansion, prosperity, recession, and depression. Then it repeats itself. Real estate prices are greatly influenced by the economic cycle. Typically, real estate is said to do well in the expansion and prosperity phases and poorly in the recession and depression phases.

The real estate market is cyclical. It always has been cyclical. It always will be cyclical. This means the real estate market expands, levels off, contracts, bottoms out, and expands again. Because of inflation, today's bottom of the market is always higher than yesterday's bottom of the market.

As we demonstrated with the property that Bill bought in 1976 and sold in 1979, the real estate market's expectation of future inflation drives real estate prices upward beyond the actual inflation rates. What do you think the inflation rates are going to be over the next 10, 15, or 20 years?

Don't you wish you had bought more real estate 10, 15, or 20 years ago? Project yourself out 10, 15, or 20 years in the future. Look back from the future. Aren't you glad you bought all that real estate 20, 15, and 10 years ago? We know we are!

As you go forward in your various investing adventures continue learning and developing yourself. Maybe we will see you in one of our classes at Howell Carey International University. As we always say, we want to hear from you about your progress!

We have been training staff to better assist you at getting to us in a timely manner for your fee-based consulting, partnering, and educational fulfillment requests. We can currently be reached via e-mail to either thetrustee@hotmail.com or hciu_edu@yahoo.com. Stay tuned for a new web site to be launched.

Congratulations on your success!

# INDEX

Main entries are boldfaced for your convenience.